Southwestern American Indian Literature

American Indian Studies

Elizabeth Hoffman Nelson and Malcolm A. Nelson
General Editors

Vol. 17

PETER LANG
New York • Washington, D.C./Baltimore • Bern
Frankfurt am Main • Berlin • Brussels • Vienna • Oxford

CONRAD SHUMAKER

Southwestern American Indian Literature

In the Classroom and Beyond

PETER LANG
New York • Washington, D.C./Baltimore • Bern
Frankfurt am Main • Berlin • Brussels • Vienna • Oxford

Library of Congress Cataloging-in-Publication Data

Shumaker, Conrad.
Southwestern American Indian literature: in the classroom and beyond /
Conrad Shumaker.
p. cm. — (American Indian studies; v. 17)
Includes bibliographical references.
1. American literature—Indian authors—History and criticism.
2. American literature—Indian authors—Study and teaching.
3. Indians of North America—Southwestern States—Intellectual life.
4. American literature—Southwestern States—History and criticism.
5. Indian literature—Study and teaching—United States.
6. Southwestern States—In literature. 7. Indians in literature. I. Title.
PS153.I52S55   810.9'897—dc22   2007005853
ISBN 978-0-8204-6344-5
ISSN 1058-563X

Bibliographic information published by **Die Deutsche Bibliothek**.
Die Deutsche Bibliothek lists this publication in the "Deutsche
Nationalbibliografie"; detailed bibliographic data is available
on the Internet at http://dnb.ddb.de/.

Cover photo by Celia Bernheimer

© 2008 Peter Lang Publishing, Inc., New York
29 Broadway, 18th floor, New York, NY 10006
www.peterlang.com

All rights reserved.
Reprint or reproduction, even partially, in all forms such as microfilm,
xerography, microfiche, microcard, and offset strictly prohibited.

Contents

Acknowledgments vii

Chapter 1: Learning from Literature 1

Chapter 2: Beginnings:
The Stories and Poems of Simon Ortiz 13

Chapter 3: Putting a World Together
Teaching Leslie Marmon Silko's *Ceremony* 23

Chapter 4: "Made of Prayers"
Luci Tapahonso and Navajo Culture 39

Chapter 5: The Quiet People
George Webb's *A Pima Remembers* and the Akimel O'odham 57

Chapter 6: American Indian Literature as World Literature
"Yellow Woman" and *Smoke Signals* 71

Chapter 7: Out of the Classroom and into the Canyons
An American Indian Travel Course in Theory and Practice 85

Notes 107

Works Cited 113

Further Readings 117

Acknowledgments

This study would not have been possible without the help of a large number of people. Perhaps the most important are those Acoma, Navajo, Hopi, and Pima individuals who have contributed to my travel seminars, for they invited us to visit their homes, share their food, learn from their cultures, and share the experience of being on the land with us. Their help enabled me to see American Indian literatures and cultures in ways that would not have been possible otherwise, and their influence informs this book from start to finish. Many thanks to Dale Sanchez, who has introduced us to Acoma culture with skill and humor; Sunny Dooley, who meets us at Canyon De Chelly and comes to Conway to share Navajo stories and lives up to her name by bringing light to everyone who meets her; Dave Wilson and Percy Begay, who have led us into Canyon De Chelly and shared stories about its role in Navajo history and their own lives with us; Ray Coin and Susan and Dorothy Secakaku, who have guided us at Hopi and shared work time, meals, and recipes with us; Michael Kabotie, who has inspired us with his artistic talent and his knowledge of Hopi art and life, as well as his trickster's sense of humor; Ramona and Terry Button, who give us insight into Pima culture and generosity; and Bobby Stone, who continues to inspire with his skill as a farm manager, his insights about how we learn, and his ideas for the water that the Pima people are getting back.

I would also like to thank the staff members at the Museum of Northern Arizona for their invaluable help in setting up the travel course, especially Tracy Anderson, Lisa Lamberson, and Don Keller. They have been consistently helpful, cheerful, and cool-headed in the midst of crisis, and their ability to provide expert guidance, reassure frightened students, and respond to crises has been an inspiration.

Elaine Fox and Stella Capek, Professors of Sociology at UCA and Hendrix, respectively, helped me set up the travel course and have contributed to its continuation, and I would like to thank the many students who have braved temperature extremes, altitude sickness, culture shock, and days without showers to survive the trips and to teach me a great deal along the way.

I would especially like to thank Heidi Burns, my editor at Peter Lang Publisning, who has been helpful and patient as this project developed, and the general series editor, Elizabeth Hoffman Nelson, whose enthusiasm for my presentations at several American Culture Association conferences gave me the hope that I might be able to undertake a book project.

An earlier version of chapter 3 appeared in *Telling the Stories,* ed. Elizabeth Hoffman-Nelson and Malcom Nelson (Peter Lang, 2001), and an earlier version of chapter 7 appeared in *Studies in American Indian Literatures,* ser. 2, 19 (2007). I would like to thank the editors of both those publications for their help in developing my ideas.

Finally, thank you to Sara, companion on the road and at home, critic, teacher, and supporter, without whom none of this could happen.

Chapter 1

Learning from Literature

Learning from versus Learning about

This book will present a thesis that seems obvious yet is quite complex in its cultural implications: As European Americans, students and teachers, we need to learn from the indigenous cultures of this land. Our history seems to have left us thoroughly confused about this issue. As a people, we of European American culture[1] are very good at learning *about* other cultures, nature, and the universe. The record shows very little evidence, though, that we can learn *from* them. This is a crucial distinction. To learn about, as I use the term here, is to approach another being as an object (to use Martin Buber's famous distinction, to have an "I-it" relationship). To learn from is to approach another as an equal, even as having superior knowledge in some areas. It is to enter into a very different relationship, to engage, to listen, to accept and respect the other's living humanity, and, ultimately, even to change the way we do things in response to what we find.

An experience I had in Sedona, Arizona, might begin to make this distinction clearer. I was leading a group of students enrolled in a travel seminar: We had met with a Navajo storyteller and Hopi elders, scholars, and artists. We had hiked into Canyon De Chelly with Dave Wilson, a Navajo guide who told us about his family's history there; we had shared a traditional meal with a Hopi family in the village of Bacavi and had plastered a house using mud and our hands in order to prepare it for a ceremony. Hopi villagers had stopped to thank us for our work as they passed by, and we had returned their gratitude. Now we were on our way to the Gila River reservation to meet with Pima (Akimel O'odham) people—some very successful farmers who would give us a tour of their farms and join us in a traditional Pima meal. Along the way we had spent time discussing works by contemporary Southwestern writers such as Leslie Marmon Silko, Luci Tapahonso, Simon Ortiz, and the Pima writer, George Webb. While we were gassing up our two vans in Sedona, a middle-aged man came over to chat with me and ask what we were doing. I gave him a brief explanation, and he asked me if we had visited the ruins at Mesa Verde—a question I am asked regularly in connection with this course. "Actually," I said (once again), "Mesa Verde is a really interesting place, but we're more focused on meeting people from the living cultures." I could see a wall come up between us. "If you want to see the living cultures," he said, "go to the casino." Then he turned and walked away.

Mesa Verde, Chaco Canyon, Montezuma Castle—most people assume that a travel seminar in Southwest American Indian cultures should focus on such places. Those are the places people want to talk about and ask about when I tell them about the course. We are much more comfortable with dead cultures, even when they insist, like the plague victim in *Monty Python and the Holy Grail*, that they are very much alive and feeling better. By assuming that a culture is dead we can learn about it without having to engage with the human complexity that makes interaction more difficult. The man at the station in Sedona was prepared to admire ruins and learn about the lives of "vanished" people, but he was not willing to engage living people whose ways are different from his.

There are, of course, much more subtle versions of this attitude than the one we encountered in Sedona. Romanticizing "Indians" is one of the more prevalent: "That's my last warrior hanging on the wall, looking as if he were alive . . . ." Sometimes even thoughtful students who take the travel seminar are scandalized to see that Acoma people wear Nike T-shirts, that our Navajo guide complains about tribal government, that a Hopi educator uses powerpoint to talk about the migration stories, that Pima farmers are not using organic methods. American Indians are not supposed to be struggling with or adapting to American culture the way we are. How can they be models for us if they are not static and tranquil and completely "natural"? How can we admire them properly if they are struggling with change and modern developments judst as we are, instead of remaining solemnly aloof from all that?

Confronting this problem makes putting together a course on American Indian literature quite tricky. How do we treat stories that were collected by anthropologists who believed that they were "saving" the tales as relics of a vanishing people, for example? Can we learn from those stories and still acknowledge the tensions inherent in trying to transfer an oral tradition to print and in treating a living culture as if its traditions can be boxed and sold? The "as told to" autobiographies offer similar problems: Though *Black Elk Speaks* is certainly a great book (as Vine Deloria, Jr., argues eloquently in his introduction to the Bison Books edition), it also embodies the "vanishing Indian" syndrome in Neihardt's expurgation of Black Elk's Catholicism and bawdiness, and students need to know about the controversy around the book. Similarly, to teach Silko's *Ceremony* without engaging the cultural struggles within the book and around the book (e.g., the controversies over changing the ceremonies within the novel and the controversies with Paula Gunn Allen and Louise Erdrich over the role of the American Indian writer) is to leave out some of the human complexity. Moreover, writers such as Simon Ortiz demand that we respond to the stories by taking action. It is not enough to admire his literary skills; he asks us to fight oppression and exploitation along with his Acoma people, and to ignore that demand is to misrepresent him as a writer.

In short, if we are really dealing with living cultures, we have to deal with change, controversy, and struggle, as well as with traditions, stories, and ceremonies that have persisted. My approach here, then, is to see the literature as part of a dynamic process of growth and change. I want to focus on the ways in which the works force us to grapple with a confrontation between traditional cultures and "America" with all its assumptions, for if we fail to appreciate the ways in which American Indians are responding to American culture—to the same things we have to struggle with—we will miss much of what there is to learn.

This is crucial. If nothing else, we need to understand that everything we as European Americans have done to American Indians, we have also done to ourselves. In the name of private property and efficient land use (which is actually supremely destructive and inefficient), we drove native peoples off the land that they had settled and lived on for hundreds or even thousands of years, and then we did the same to most of our own farmers. We did what we could to undermine family structure and traditions by educating American Indians to desire participation in the individualistic American dream, and we've done the same to ourselves. We polluted and destroyed their land and water sources in order to obtain mineral wealth and, more recently, to dispose of our waste, and in the process we did the same to our own. We replaced a traditional diet based on healthy local foods with an exploitive one based on profit for the food industry, causing widespread malnutrition, obesity, and diabetes, and we are now discovering that we have done the same to ourselves. As Wendell Berry points out, Europeans didn't "settle" America; we unsettled it. After uprooting the peoples who were already settled here, we continued the process by dispossessing, exploiting, and driving out those among us who found a home with the land. As Berry puts it, "[T]he members of any *established* people or group or community sooner or later become 'redskins'—that is, they become the designated victims of an utterly ruthless, officially sanctioned and subsidized exploitation" (original emphasis).[2] In *Ceremony*, Leslie Marmon Silko uses the Pueblo concept of "witchery" to put forward a very similar idea. The main character, Tayo, recognizes that the whites who stole Mount Taylor become the ultimate victims of the forces they serve: Those who refuse to see that our culture was built on stolen land will become the victims of the witchery: "they would never know that they were still being manipulated by those who knew how to stir the ingredients together."[3] Until we understand what American Indian peoples (among others) have to tell us about the land, the stories, and ourselves, we will continue to be all-too-willing victims of this process. As Simon Ortiz puts it in *Woven Stone*, "If the survival and quality of life of Indian peoples is not assured, then no one else's life is, because those same economic, social, and political forces which destroy them will surely destroy others."[4]

So, to turn to the positive side of the question, what does it mean to learn *from* American Indian literature and cultures? That is a long story—it is what the rest of the book is about. I can, however, offer a suggestive model and a brief discussion here. One of the highlights of our visit to the Acoma Pueblo in 2004 and again in 2006 was the Catholic church. Our guide, Dale Sanchez, made it come alive for us. She talked about the dirt floor as connecting the worshippers to the earth, pointed out that it is never swept entirely clean, since the dust is the body of our mother, explained the connection between the Corn Mother and the Virgin Mary, called our attention to the rainbows, the parrots, and the sun symbols on the walls, and made offerings of water to the earth as she entered the church and again as she approached the altar. She told us how the infant Christ rests in a cradle that is touched by sunlight from an east window on the fourth day after his birth so that he, like any Acoma child, can be presented to his Sun Father. She did not gloss over the struggles that came with Catholicism, the abuses by the Spanish before and after the Pueblo Rebellion, the children who were forced into slavery in exchange for one of the church's bells, or the hardships of bringing roof timbers from Mt. Taylor. Nevertheless, she made it very clear for us that this place, a living incarnation of tradition, struggle, and change, is an intensely holy symbol of human life and worship in relationship with the earth, the animals and plants—and with what is best in other cultures.

One kind of purist might deplore the watering down of Christianity by Acoma "superstitions." Can't we keep our religions safely within their cultural corrals? Another kind might object that the church represents the "contamination" of Acoma culture by Christianity. Certainly, we should not underestimate the damage done to native peoples in the name of a Christianity that often attempted to make them ashamed of their traditions and stories. The relationship is a complex and disputed one, but one of the students spoke for me as we left the church at Acoma: "This is where I want to go to church," she said. I knew she did not just mean the building. What she had in mind, I think, was the conversation— the "learning from"—embodied in that place. The Acoma people who accepted the church did not just become Catholics. They engaged Catholicism from within the strength of their own traditions, and because their traditions allow for growth, the result is a living, breathing present. This, I think, is something of what Silko has in mind when she stresses the "speckled" quality of the cattle (and the hazel-eyed people) who offer a way toward healing in *Ceremony*. This conversation between different ways of seeing represents, in fact, the present that American Indian writers are exploring, engaging, and struggling with, this present in all its tension and harshness and beauty; and the process of engagement is one of the things they have to teach us about. If we truly want to learn from these peoples, we have to treat their cultures as living, growing creations, not as static institutions that can only be contaminated by change.

Bob Housas, an Apache sculptor who has the last word in the segment on the Southwest peoples in the Turner Network's series, *The Native Americans*, gives us the other side of this valuable coin. European Americans should not put on feathers and beads and try to be Indians, he says. Every tradition has within it a sense of the holiness of the earth and all its beings, and we should find within our own traditions the place where we lost that sense. Go back there, he says, and find and nurture that. If we as European Americans try to become "Indians" we are in danger of participating in cultural appropriation and fraud, whether consciously or unconsciously, but if we are determined to learn from American Indian cultures we can grow in awareness of our own culture's strengths and weaknesses.

Literature as One Story

Paradoxically, then, studying American Indian literature can play a very important role in this process of rediscovering our own traditions, if it really is the engagement of one living culture with another; for such engagement, I would argue, always leads to our seeing our own culture with new eyes. Students who read Simon Ortiz or Leslie Marmon Silko learn to look at their own lives and ideas differently, to see things they have overlooked or to understand things they thought they knew in different ways. This brings up another important point: We cannot teach American Indian literature as if it were completely separate from "American literature" or "World literature." In "Tradition and the Individual Talent," T. S. Eliot points out that every work of literature changes the whole of literature. I think that most American Indian writers would agree—every story becomes part of, changes, and adds to the story, contributes to the making of the world through a story that is always The Story but is constantly growing. The modern-day narrator in Leslie Marmon Silko's "Yellow Woman" learns that her story is the story of Yellow Woman from ancient Pueblo tradition, and that the Yellow Woman story grows to include her reliving of it in a world of school buses and Jello. Silko's retelling of the story adds both to American Literature and to the Pueblo tradition of Yellow Woman. In recent interviews, the Navajo poet Esther Belin lists Maxine Hong Kingston and Emily Dickinson as major literary influences,[5] and Luci Tapahonso, also Navajo, mentions Tillie Olsen, Flannery O'Connor, and James Wright as important influences;[6] Simon Ortiz also mentions the importance of American and British authors in his education.[7] Moreover, as I will try to show later, teaching *Ceremony* has changed the way I think about American Literature—about Henry David Thoreau and Ralph Ellison and Amy Tan—and the way I think about teaching in general, not to mention the way I think about my own life story.

As long as we limit the study of these literatures to the classroom, to studies of literatures and cultures solely, we miss an important point. In her introduction to a special issue of *Studies of American Indian Literatures* devoted to Simon Ortiz, Susan Berry Brill De Ramirez characterizes the essays in the issue as sharing three common elements: a commitment to bettering the world and people's lives, a sense of "the harmony and power of orality and storytelling," and an "engagement with the sacred." She concludes her introduction by pointing out that Ortiz's writing "encourages us all toward a creative writing and scholarship that is integrally invested in the good of the world."[8] This, I would argue, is the real "cutting edge," the direction that our teaching of this literature should take: We should encourage students to look beyond the classroom, to see how American Indian literatures (and, by extension, literature in general) can change the way we are in the world, can clarify the stories by which we live.

My own experience might once again serve as an illustration here. I managed to get a Ph.D. in American Literature without reading a single work of American Indian literature. This was not entirely the fault of the institutions where I studied: Both the University of Arizona and UCLA had among their faculty a pioneer in the field. American Indian literature, however, was exactly that—"a field"—a speciality that seemed to have little to do with my own academic concerns. When I discovered American Indian writers by team-teaching a class with another professor who was interested in the subject, it was a revelation to me. The story of my life changed.

I had grown up on 750 acres of cotton farm, cow pasture, and Sonoran desert outside Tucson, acres that I knew intimately from walking over them, from plowing and planting, riding horses and working cattle. The last time I visited that place, it was mostly a gravel pit half a mile wide and over a hundred feet deep. All the fields, the arroyos, the mesquite trees, the saguaros, had been bulldozed, dug up, loaded and trucked into Tucson to build streets and banks and stores and houses for people coming from other places, many of which were being treated in similar ways. All I could find of my family's history there was a strand of rusty barbed wire stretched between two lone mesquite trees and a small pile of adobe melting into the sand and the treated sewage of the Santa Cruz River. Reading Navajo, Pueblo, Cherokee, Lakota stories gave me a new way of seeing and saying that experience. I understood in a new way why I felt outside mainstream American culture with its story of hard work and material gain, of dominion over nature and conquering the wilderness. Over time it gave me a feeling that I could do something about it.

Indeed, there are times when I wish I could become a Hopi or a Navajo, in spite of what I know about the difficulty of reservation life, and I truly understand the impulse that leads many European Americans to put on feathers and beads and try to become Indians, to paraphrase Bob Housas. However, I think I engage more truly with the literature when I plant squash and corn in my own garden or when I work with students in the community garden that we started as a result of the travel seminar in American Indian Literatures, or when I get my students to discover connections between Thoreau and Silko, Ortiz and Barbara Kingsolver, to look at and rethink their own stories based on those connections, and then to decide what they might do about it.

Why Southwestern Literature?

In this time of the "American Indian Renaissance," there is certainly a wealth of American Indian literature that rewards close study. One of the hardest parts of preparing a course these days is deciding what to leave out. Choices must be made, however, and I have chosen to focus on the literature of this region for what seem to me to be good reasons.

First, the traditional way of life is more fully intact in the Southwest than in many other areas of the United States. Because of a number of factors—the remoteness of the area; the unattractiveness of "barren deserts" to early settlers; the military or cultural resistance of tribes such as the Hopi, Apache, and Navajo; and some successful adaptations by the Pima and Pueblo peoples, for example—many cultures in the area have managed to protect their land and keep their traditions alive and well. Several villages have been continuously inhabited for hundreds of years and the ceremonial life there has gone on largely unbroken (though often with difficulty and underground). The Indian Health Services hospital in Chinle, Arizona, to give one remarkable example, has on its staff a Navajo singer and on its grounds a traditional Navajo hogan that is used for ceremonies as part of the health care system. The native languages are often taught to children, and radio broadcasts in Navajo and Hopi reflect the importance of those languages and help to keep them actively spoken. Survival of the language is a very important factor, one that is mentioned by such writers as Simon Ortiz and Luci Tapahonso as crucial to a continuing sense of identity.

In addition, the issues that confront Americans in general as we try to understand American Indians—land use, exploitation of minerals and water, views of success, treatment of animals, views of religion, and so on—are highlighted and defined in the Southwest in ways that students can readily understand (with a little help). The deadly effects of uranium mining and processing (the uranium mine is an important symbol for both Ortiz and Silko), the theft of Salt River and Gila River water from the Pimas, the destruction of Navajo and Hopi land, water, and shrines by the Peabody Coal Company, the clumsy attempts to resolve the dispute over the so-called joint-use area, all help to define the ways in which Americans have abused, ignored, or misunderstood these peoples, and they define sharply the issues that divide the American Indian way of seeing the world from the mainstream American way. At the same time, the peoples in the area have been able to adapt and survive, finding ways of incorporating aspects of western culture through their own traditions, thus offering many examples of the dynamic nature of American Indian traditions I referred to earlier.

I also focus on the Southwest because that is the terrain I know and love. Having grown out of the deserts and mountains myself, and having taken several groups of students out to experience the land and meet the people, I think I can create a context for the literature that will help those who want to teach it, either by itself or as part of a wider ranging syllabus.

A Practical Approach

This work is intended to be practical rather than theoretical. I understand that it is not always easy to differentiate between the two, that any approach, however practical, must be informed by some kind of theoretical framework, whether it is stated or not. I tend to agree with the "New Historicism" that literature can fruitfully be studied as one way of joining the conversation about the meaning of history, making a claim for a particular version of what history is and how it gets told. I think that much could be written on that topic when it comes to American Indian literature, and that a New Historical approach might illuminate many of the issues that the literature addresses. A careful reader will discover, in fact, that such an approach governs my reading of the literature in many ways. In this work, however, I limit my focus to confronting particular challenges in the classroom. How do we get students to understand the injustices in America's treatment of its Native peoples without making them feel that American Indians are hostile toward all whites and do not want us to learn from their traditions? How do we overcome the contradiction inherent in "analyzing" a literature that speaks out against the very approach to the world that is inherent in the process of analysis? How do we confront student perceptions that American Indians see themselves as victims? How do we expand the world literature course to include American Indian literature without oversimplifying the literature or confusing students with an incoherent tour of world cultures? How do we become aware of and learn to question the cultural assumptions that are built into the very spaces in which we teach? Each chapter centers on one of those practical considerations and offers approaches that have developed from actual teaching and from leading travel courses.

As for my choice of subjects, I have tried to combine the established figures such as Simon Ortiz and Leslie Marmon Silko with some less well known writers. Luci Tapahonso's work is being discovered and taught more widely, but I think there is room to help make her better known. George Webb's book, *A Pima*

Remembers is a bit of a special case. It has been in print since 1959, but it deserves a wider readership. I received a copy from my father, who was given it by Cameron Webb, George Webb's grandson. Cameron and I became friends when we worked construction together, and he was planning to take me to some of the places discussed in the book before his untimely death. I have had much success teaching the book and would like to make a case for its inclusion in an American Indian literature syllabus in spite of its deceptively simple style and approach. Like the Pima people themselves, *A Pima Remembers* has much more to say than appears on the surface.

I have included a discussion of one work that is not from the Southwest and is not strictly literature. *Smoke Signals*, with its screenplay by Sherman Alexie, works so well in my World Literature course when I teach it in conjunction with Silko's "Yellow Woman" (a widely anthologized work), that I would like to make a pitch for incorporating the two—together or separately—as part of a truly inclusive World Literature class. I have also included a chapter on the theory and practice of the travel seminar in American Indian Literature. Designing and leading the travel course has been one of the most challenging and rewarding things I have done, and, for me and for most of the students who participate, it is a life-changing experience. Therefore I would like to share what I have learned in the hope that others might try a similar approach.

Ultimately this book is about inclusion, change, and the examination of assumptions. I want my students to understand that American Indians are part of our world, however much we try in our different ways to relegate them to the past. I want them to understand that successful cultures are dynamic and changing and cannot be contained in museums, national parks, or anthropological studies. As Diane Glancy puts it in her poem, "He Has More Than One Ear," among other things American Indian literatures and cultures teach us that "it's transformation that is the constant."[9] Finally, I want them to understand the conclusion that Glancy comes to in her poem:

> NA Lit and culture offer you the seventh direction
> after North, East, South, West, Earth, Sky
> there's Center
>
> Which is the core of yourself
> you carry with you wherever you go.[10]

In gaining a better understanding of these traditions, we also gain a clearer sense of those human qualities that our culture does not always acknowledge or honor, and a clearer sense of the ways in which we cannot ignore or denigrate those human qualities in other traditions without losing touch with and doing damage to ourselves.

Chapter 2

Beginnings: The Stories and Poems of Simon Ortiz

Grappling with the Real Issues

Teaching American Indian literature presents challenges and pitfalls that are not always present in other areas of study. A major villain in Sherman Alexie's *Indian Killer* illustrates some of the potential problems: He is a professor who manages to teach a course on Native literature without exposing the students to a single work actually written by an American Indian. His texts include such works as *Black Elk Speaks*, *The Education of Little Tree*, and a mystery novel by a writer who falsely claims to be an Indian through descent from an obscure tribe. This choice of works enables the professor to avoid the hard questions and issues that contemporary American Indian literature raises, and when Marie Polatkin, a Spokane Indian student, asks why they are not looking at contemporary writers and issues, the professor responds that he is just trying to "present a positive portrait of Indian peoples, of your people."[1] The character is (I hope) something of a caricature, yet he serves as a sobering reminder of some questions we have to ask as we think about teaching this body of literature. First, how can we make students aware of political issues such as cultural oppression and the appropriation of tradition that masks itself as sympathy for native peoples? How can we present American Indian cultures, not as artifacts preserved by anthropologists, but as living, growing, and diverse ways of life which are subject to oppression and struggle (with both internal and external forces) here and now? Finally, how can we do all this without giving students the equally inaccurate impression that we are unqualified to study the literature or that native peoples resent any attempt to learn from their traditions and culture?

In this chapter I would like to offer Simon Ortiz's poetry and stories as an aid to negotiating this tricky territory, a way of raising important questions and defining key issues that are central to the study of American Indian literature, and at the same time focusing on what the traditions have to offer.

Born on the Acoma reservation in Deetseyamah (or McCarty's, New Mexico, on U.S. maps, named for the Irishman who sold Acoma water to trains passing through the reservation), Ortiz has seen, experienced, and written about many of the outrages suffered by southwestern native peoples—the appropriation of land by the railroad and by American speculators, the destruction of land and lives by the mining industry, the effects of racism and exploitation on Indians who try to find work with American companies or in American towns, the destruction caused by alcoholism, and the insensitivity of whites who come to the reservations or VA hospitals looking for "real Indians." Ortiz names these sins in a direct effort to get people to *Fight Back*—that is the title of his 1980 collection of poems. The rest of the title, however, reveals the deeper concern present in all his writing—*For the Sake of the People, For the Sake of the Land*. The subtitle reminds us of what I have heard from the Acoma and Hopi educators I have spoken with—in the Pueblo traditions "the People" means all the people. Whatever our race or background, we depend on the land and on a cycle of receiving and giving back that keeps the people and the land both alive. Pueblo ceremonies are meant to continually reestablish this cycle for the sake of everyone. Ortiz wants us as "Mericanos" to acknowledge the destruction we participate in, but he also invites us to learn from Pueblo tradition and to join the struggle against those who exploit all of us by using the land without respecting and giving back to it. In what follows here, I will look at both sides of Ortiz's message to suggest that, through his works, we can introduce students to the problems we find in the study of this literature and at the same time show them the real value of learning from these traditions. I will begin by highlighting the poems and essays in *Woven Stone* in which Ortiz chronicles his people's struggles and then turn to two stories in *Men on the Moon*, in which he suggests ways in which Acoma traditions can teach us "Mericanos" something about healing and our own relationship to the land.

"The Wisconsin Horse"

We can see just how effectively Ortiz evokes the oppression suffered by the Acoma (and by American Indian peoples in general) by tracing the themes in the three collections of poems brought together in the volume entitled *Woven Stone*. In his first book, *Going for the Rain*, Ortiz presents an image that will recur often in later poems—"The Wisconsin Horse," which stands behind a fence not far from a construction site. "I tell I tell the horse," Ortiz writes, "'That's America building something.'"[2] Standing within a fence while America builds something is a telling metaphor for the Acoma experience, and much of Ortiz's writing details just what it is that America builds and how it has led to the fence around the "*Aacqumeh hanoh*," as Ortiz refers to his people. Indeed, his description of the experience of the Acoma can stand as a telling illustration of the kinds of things that happened to the Southwestern peoples in general. Students are generally aware of the "Indian wars," but they do not often understand the subtler kinds of struggles faced by American Indian peoples. In the essay that concludes *Woven Stone*—"Our Homeland, A National Sacrifice Area"—Ortiz chronicles the theft of traditional Acoma land, first by the railroads and then by settlers and speculators. He puts this development in the context of the Spanish arrival, the Pueblo Revolt of 1680, and the return of the Spanish on somewhat less tyrannical terms in 1692. The people managed heroically to resist, survive, and even flourish under the direct assault mounted by the Spanish. However, when the Americans arrived, things were not as clear. The "Mericano" onslaught was quite different:

> The Aacqumeh hanoh had never seen thieves like the Mericano before. They were so shrewd, talkative, even helpful, and so friendly they didn't look like thieves. As the Mericano stole unto the land, claiming it, the people didn't even feel like it was being taken away from them. And they even blamed themselves and began to feel it was their fault.[3]

This sense of self-blame and the inability to see just how the land was being stolen left the Acoma with a sense of hopelessness that they hadn't felt before. The people lost the memory of the courageous struggle against Spanish domination, Ortiz says, "and they felt only a stasis that could not name an enemy though surely there was one."[4] This self-blame is an important issue in American Indian literature. The idea that the people somehow did something wrong to bring about the loss of the land that supported their way of life is present in works from *Black Elk Speaks* to *Ceremony*, and it contributes to a loss of self-respect and identity.

Meanwhile, Indian schools were working overtly to eliminate Pueblo languages and traditions: In the Preface to *Woven Stone* Ortiz calls the BIA schools "a severe and traumatic form of brainwashing," designed quite openly to separate children from their traditional heritage and identity in order to make "Americans" of them.[5]

These strategies, rooted in the American belief in "Manifest Destiny," the belief that American culture had a divine mandate to conquer all the "primitive" peoples in the path of western settlement, left the Acoma with little choice except to work for the railroads and then the mining companies that had taken the land. Work on the railroads took men away from their families, further contributing to the weakening of Acoma traditions and family structure. In a poem with the ominous title of "Final Solution: Jobs, Leaving," Ortiz captures the feeling of a child waiting for the return of a father whose railroad job has taken him away:

> Hearts.
> Blood. Bones and skin. Love
> and hope. O Daddy. Please train.[6]

The image of the train and the desperate feeling for a loved one who left by train and may be lost forever suggest an allusion to the Holocaust, and Ortiz wants us to understand that the policies that forced the men off the reservation were grounded in the same claims of cultural and racial superiority that justified Hitler's attempt to eradicate the "undesirables" in 1940s Germany. In the name of "Manifest Destiny," forced assimilation, termination (the efforts to end federal protection of and assistance to reservations in the 1940s and 1950s), and relocation (moving Indian peoples off their traditional lands in order to force their assimilation into mainstream society) were meant in one way or another to be America's "Final Solution" to the "Indian Problem."

Remembering the desperation he felt as a child and his father's admonition never to work for the railroad, Ortiz took a job in the uranium mines near Grants, only to find that the mines had their own deadly hazards. Workers were not told anything about the danger of handling uranium or "yellowcake," the processed form of the ore, and many of them developed cancer from their work in the mines and refineries. When the mineshafts were sunk below the water table, they filled with water which was pumped into desert washes. The contaminated water seeped into underground aquifers, making creeks, springs, and rivers hazardous because of radiation levels.

Pueblo and Navajo people were not the only victims: Miners from states such as West Virginia and Oklahoma came to New Mexico to work and were subjected to similar exploitation and hazardous conditions. When these more experienced workers organized strikes to protest low wages and hazardous conditions, the mine bosses hired Indians out of the jails in Grants and Gallup to replace striking workers. Ortiz recalls the situation in a poem entitled, "Indians Sure Came in Handy." The jailed Indians became a resource for mine bosses who were breaking the strike—to the extent that jailers would "call in sick" for prisoners and tell them which mines were hiring.

> The unions didn't have much of a chance,
> and Grants just kept on booming.[7]

Once the unions were broken, of course, the Indians went back to jail, but now they had company. In a poem ironically entitled "Affirmative Action," Ortiz observes that the new and larger jail in Grants "filled/with Cajuns, Okies, Mexicans, Blacks,/as well as Indians" (303). It is this version of "Affirmative Action" that Ortiz calls us to recognize and fight against in the essay that concludes *Woven Stone*. The experience of the Acoma, he insists, reflects the experience of all the people of this country: "If the survival and quality of life of Indian peoples is not assured, then no one else's life is, because those same economic, social, and political forces which destroy them will surely destroy others."[8] He ends his essay by calling on all of us to recognize our part in the battle: "Only when the people of this nation, not just Indian people, fight for what is just and good for all life, will we know life and its continuance."[9]

To sum up, then, leading students through the poems and essays in *Woven Stone* is an excellent way to get them to grapple with the issues involved in the study of American Indian literature, and to see the power of a contemporary writer as he explores those issues through his own experiences and art. It can also show students that we must struggle with these issues, not just because we owe it to American Indian people (though that is reason enough), but because everyone's survival depends on the awareness that Ortiz is calling for.

"To Change Life in a Good Way"

The university where I teach is connected to McCarty's, New Mexico, by

Interstate 40, by the railroad, which regularly delays the students as they drive across town, and by the main source of our electricity—a nuclear power plant about 50 miles west up the Arkansas River. Thanks to Ortiz's works, it is thus easy to show the students in my classes just how completely we are connected to the Pueblo and Navajo peoples as we sit in our desks and discuss literature under light generated in part by uranium which might be taken from Pueblo and Navajo land by exploited workers. I think it is crucial for students to think about such things as part of their education. I want them to understand that right now, as we go about our daily lives, we are participating in a system that continues to benefit from the destruction of American Indian land and traditions. Simon Ortiz makes a concrete understanding of that possible in very effective ways.

At the same time, I am not a believer in the efficacy of collective guilt. An African American professor with whom I team taught for many years showed me what I think is a much better response to the situation. When white students in our class would express their feeling of guilt over their ancestors' participation in slavery, Patricia McGraw would say in the most emphatic terms, "Don't feel guilty. You weren't there. You're here. What will you do now?"

To put the question in terms of this literature, what can we learn from writers like Ortiz that will help us understand and address the situation here and now? It seems to me that education fully serves its purpose only when it helps us deal with such questions. If, for example, it teaches us about the characteristics of Pueblo culture or the use of symbolism in contemporary American Indian writers without challenging us to see how those relate to the way we live our lives, I think it leaves something to be desired. In other words, if our students learn *about* American Indian literature (or British or American literature) without learning *from* it, I think we have failed them. This does not mean that literature should be didactic or presented as moral lessons. Rather than giving us formulas in language that prescribe a way of living, literature opens us up. It challenges our assumptions, presents us with action and imagery that canot be reduced to cliché or a moral, and therefore asks us to deal with a view of life that we have not encountered before.

With that in mind, I would like to focus on two stories from *Men on the Moon* in which Ortiz specifically addresses the question of connections in very interesting ways. Both stories are narrated from the point of view, not of Indian people, but of working-class whites who are encountering Indian people and reacting to the encounter, the kind of people Ortiz came to know during his time as a mine worker. The first, "To Change Life in a Good Way," was published as a poem in *Fight Back* and then reprinted as a prose piece in *Men on the*

Moon, a collection of stories published in 1999. The narrative center of the story is a mine worker from Oklahoma named, simply, Bill. Living in a trailer with his wife Ida and working in the uranium mines as an electrician's helper, Bill makes friends with a Pueblo man named Pete, and eventually he and Ida become friends with Pete's wife Mary as well. Significantly, the description of this friendship centers largely around Bill and Ida's garden. Pete and Mary give advice and provide sheep manure so that the white couple can connect more successfully with the land.

The story takes a turn when Bill's younger brother Slick is killed because he steps on an American mine in Vietnam. Pete and Mary comfort Bill and give him an ear of corn and a cornhusk bundle that contains ceremonial objects— cedar sticks, beads, cotton, pollen, tobacco. Pete explains the significance of the gifts as Bill is preparing to leave for Oklahoma to attend Slick's funeral. The corn is to plant "to know that life will keep on."[10] Pete goes on to say that he does not know everything about the bundle, does not even know whether he has made it correctly in the traditional way. Nevertheless, he says, it is important for them to receive and use the bundle. Bill and Ida are not Indian, he continues, but it does not really make any difference. The bundle is "for all of us." Bill must take it and put it "someplace important that you think might be good, maybe to change life in a good way, that you think Slick might be helping us with."[11] This idea that a ceremony means doing things for all of us can be applied to Ortiz's writing as well. The Pueblo traditions and stories, even as they change, are there for the good of all life, and Ortiz tells his own stories with that spirit in mind.

The effect on Bill is just what we hope for in the classroom—a new way of seeing a familiar world. When he goes to Oklahoma for the funeral, he hears the old clichés about his brother's death—that he died doing his duty, that he was keeping America "[a]dvanced and safe from the Communist peril" just like people in the past who fought off Indians "to build homes on new land." The speakers of these clichés never stop to ask how they can reconcile this belief in "America" with their knowledge of the reality: They also discuss the way that the Oklahoma senator who owns the mining company is "gonna screw those folks in New Mexico just like he has here."[12] But Bill no longer hears the talk the way he has before. On the way home he thinks about Slick's death, and he finally understands "what Slick had died of and for." It was not just from being in a dangerous place and stepping on a mine, he realizes: "The reason was something else, and though Bill wasn't completely sure about it yet, he felt he was beginning to know. And he knew what he was going to do with the bundle in the cupboard."[13]

Bill takes the bundle to work and leaves it in a place underground where the company has failed to provide adequate shoring. He asks Slick to help keep them safe and explains that he has learned that "Indians are more righter than we've ever been led to believe."[14] The bundle becomes the symbol of a connection between people of different backgrounds who are the intended victims of a corrupt system, one that sacrifices the people and the land for the sake of power and greed. The Pueblo traditions, even when their exact ritual details have faded, offer a way for Bill to begin to understand and express his growing awareness that he and Ida and Slick, along with Pete and Mary, are threatened by those who prosper through exploitation and destruction. Having been awakened to the values he shares with Pete and Ida, Bill is ready to "change life in a good way" through small but significant acts. The fight against the corrupt powers that work to destroy the people and the land is not carried on in spectacular or large-scale ways. It consists of the things we do in awareness, the mundane but significant gestures that affirm our willingness to participate in a healthier view of ourselves and the land.

The story "Hiding, West of Here" is narrated by a white mine worker who "hides out" in the mountains in order to experience a connection to nature that he canot put into words. In the story's present he stumbles as he tries to explain it. Then he turns to the experience that has led him to think about the meaning of his hiding, an experience that has been shaped by his acquaintance with some of the Pueblo men he works with. They share complaints about the mines and their bosses, and sometimes the Indian workers talk about larger issues that leave the narrator feeling ambivalent: When a young Indian worker denounces the way white Americans exploit the land and leave workers vulnerable, the narrator is not sure whether he agrees or not: He characterizes the Indian's comments as "shit like that," but adds, "Which I go along with sometimes in agreement, but other times I don't." He resolves the conflict in a way that seems too easy at first but will have deeper implications by the end of the story: The Indians, he concludes, are "no different from myself and other workers who have to make a living at that kind of work."[15]

Then he goes on to tell about a ceremony he has witnessed. As he is hiding he sees two Indian men climbing the mountain towards him. Watching them carry a cornhusk bundle to a huge rock, he understands that they are doing a ceremony and praying. He feels like an interloper because it is clear that the Indians think they are alone, and yet he also feels that somehow he is supposed to be there. He realizes that his "hiding" has been a kind of prayer. "And then it seemed like I was part of what the Indians were doing. Like they wanted me to be even though they didn't know I was there."[16] This feeling of participation leads him to reflect on his boyhood in West Virginia, when he would look at the countryside, notice the way coal mining had torn it up, and imagine how it must have looked before the mines came along. "And," he says, "I'd see something that was there, the meaning of something." The two Indian men place the bundle in a crack in the rock, and the narrator understands, in a phrase that echoes his own experience, "that was the meaning of something." As he watches the Indians leave, he says, "I just felt, in fact I could see myself, like I was still hiding with the quiet and the mountain and the praying that had been going on."[17]

This story, I think, has tremendous importance for teaching American Indian literature to non-Indian students. Like the narrator, we are, in a sense, uninvited. We can feel as if we are interlopers in a world we do not understand, a world, in fact, in which people like us have played the role of oppressors. And yet, Ortiz tells us, the praying is for us too. If we can bring any kind of openness to the experience, the Pueblo traditions will speak to and for us. Our loss of connection has left us, like Ortiz's mine workers, inarticulate when it comes to expressing the feelings we might have about exploitation of people or the abuse of the land. In fact, it often seems as if our culture requires those feelings to be hidden—otherwise they will identify us as sentimental or impractical. Even most environmental organizations want to distance themselves from "tree huggers." In Pueblo tradition, however, those feelings are not only acknowledged but embodied in ceremony and in daily life. The belief in the sacredness of the land is acted out in ceremonies so that all may be reminded of their participation in the continuation of the cycles that keep us alive. Ortiz offers those traditions as a way to discover and express our own deep connections. If we have come with a willingness to learn, the stories and ceremonies will open us to new ways of seeing and will give us a way of saying what we have often felt but have not had the words for—"the meaning of something."

When I have taken students to the Southwest to meet with Pueblo, Navajo, Hopi, and Pima people, the experiences we have had affirm Ortiz's message. The people we talk to do not hesitate to tell us about the ways in which American culture has tried to destroy their traditions. Many of them have left the reservations to try living as "Americans," only to return when they find something lacking in the American dream. They often make it clear that their stories and cultural artifacts have been appropriated in ways that frustrate and anger them. They have to struggle to make a living without the land base that sustained traditional practices. Nevertheless, they welcome and honor our willingness to learn from them, and they speak for and to whatever it is in us that feels connected to the land. Consequently, the students usually return to Conway transformed and much more aware of connections. They know they cannot "be Indians," but they want to live differently. We cannot, of course, take all our students to New Mexico and Arizona, and we certainly cannot look to American Indian peoples to solve the problems we have created; but, with the help of Simon Ortiz, we can, I think, help make students aware of both the story of oppression and the possibilities for healing that Southwest American Indian literature can offer us. This is crucial. To end with Ortiz's words, "Only when the people of this nation, not just Indian people, fight for what is just and good for all life, will we know life and its continuance. And when we fight, and fight back those who are bent on destruction of land and people, we will win. We will win."[18]

Chapter 3

Putting a World Together: Teaching Leslie Marmon Silko's *Ceremony*

Transformation and Challenge

Any study of teaching Southwestern Indian literature has to include *Ceremony*, because in a way it is the book that really brought the writing of this region to national prominence. N. Scott Momaday's Pulitzer-Prize-winning *House Made of Dawn* showed that a novel by an American Indian dealing with issues central to the Southwest could be taken seriously, and it no doubt paved the way for the success of *Ceremony*. Even so, Silko's novel has had an even greater impact on readers and teachers of literature, and it displays the characteristics that make this body of literature so fascinating and valuable—the deep connection to and exploration of a particular place, the struggle between indigenous traditions and "white" ways, the focus on spirituality, to name the most prominent. My own experience, gained from teaching the novel numerous times to a variety of both undergraduate and graduate students, has suggested to me another reason for *Ceremony*'s success: It is one of those rare books that can radically change the way its readers think about the world. In the reading journals they keep in my classes, students often reveal that Silko's novel has given them a new way of seeing their own culture, allowed them to understand nature differently, or provided a language in which to express intuitions they had no words for previously. An honors student even told me that he had to stop reading one night because he realized with a sense of shock that he would not be the same person when he finished the book.

I think the work has this effect for several reasons. First, though it focuses on a Laguna man's rediscovery of his people's traditional values, it also provides a very effective criticism of European-American culture, a criticism with which many of our students can readily identify. As Virginia Kennedy argues, *Ceremony* is one of those texts that "can be used effectively in the non-Indian classroom to facilitate the 'unlearning' of established constructions implicit in the ongoing legacy of conquest."[1] Second, it offers an alternate view of the world in prose that is strikingly beautiful and deeply resonant. Finally, that vision of the world, emerging as it does from a tradition which emphasizes connection, highlights by contrast the isolation and separation our students often feel as part of their own experience. To put it in the terms I introduced at the outset, it invites students, not just to learn about Pueblo traditions and struggles, but to learn from them. It offers them a way of making sense of their own struggles with the fragmented and tangled world of twenty-first-century America.

At the same time, the book's very strengths present real challenges to anyone who would teach it. Like it or not, our approach to teaching literature has emerged from the culture the book criticizes. The problem was stated quite succinctly by a bright student the first time I taught *Ceremony*: "Why," she asked, "are we *analyzing* this book?" She had seen immediately the contradiction between the novel's emphasis on connected wholeness and an approach to literary study which has apparently borrowed from the sciences the idea that knowledge comes from "untying" the whole and studying the parts. Over the last few years I have been exploring that student's question, and this chapter, and, in a sense, this whole study, is part of that exploration. This chapter, then, will first describe and explore the view of the world Silko develops in the novel and the particular challenges that view presents. Then it will touch on some of the important symbolic milestones on Tayo's journey from fragmentation to wholeness, and finally it will suggest an approach to teaching the work that has evolved (and is still evolving) out of several years of experience. Along the way I hope to show how the challenges that *Ceremony* presents can help to clarify what we try to do when we teach literature in general.

This "Fragile" World

Silko introduces her complex view of the world most clearly near the beginning of the novel, when old Ku'oosh, a Laguna medicine man, tries to help Tayo, the mixed-blood hero of the book who is recovering from his experiences in the U.S. Army, a Japanese prisoner of war camp, and an American mental hospital. As he speaks to Tayo about the scalp ceremony, used for healing after participation in war, Ku'oosh uses "sentences that were involuted with explanations of their own origins," sentences which suggest that he is repeating things that have been said before.[2] Then he pauses. "But you know, grandson," he says, "this world is fragile." The word he uses for fragile, however, is "filled with the intricacies of a continuing process, and with a strength inherent in spider webs woven across paths through sand hills." Quite clearly, the situation is more complex than the English word can express. Because of the complexity, and the fact that "no word exists alone," Ku'oosh must explain his choice of words "with a story about why it must be said this certain way." That is what it means to be human, Ku'oosh explains, "the story behind each word must be told so there could be no mistake in the meaning of what had been said; and this demanded great patience and love."[3]

The imagery of the spider web and the emphasis on language here remind us of the book's beginning, where we are told that "Thought-Woman, the spider," is thinking of a story and that the narrator will tell us that story. Since Thought-Woman is the creator of the world, we have to understand that the world is a web, that every strand is connected to every other strand. Moreover, the stories that Thought Woman tells become reality. Throughout the novel, in fact, we are shown that the world is made of and by words and stories, which, like the spider web, catch the light in their resilient strands but can be broken. Like the strands of the web, each word or sentence has meaning only in relationship to other words, and only insofar as the teller takes the time to make sure that the listener understands the relationship between words and meanings, stories and the world. Teller and listener are connected by the love inherent in the process of understanding that language demands. The web of words forms a pattern which is different from any other yet is the same one that has been shaped countless times before. Moreover, the webs are woven across paths, which are themselves strands of a larger web, the pattern of past, present, and future journeys, the people walking on the earth. The webs on the path connect all the elements of the Pueblo world—the hills, the sun, the movement of people, the spider, the observer himself, and—through the story of Thought-Woman which the observer brings to the sight of the webs—the people and their past with its stories of the world's creation. Each part of the web participates in the strength of the whole, but the breaking of any single part will damage the whole.

It is this multi-layered sense of connections, of a fragility that is at the same time a strength, that informs Silko's novel and her view of the world. To be human is to recognize and take responsibility with patience and love for this peculiar fragility of the world and of the stories that make it.

The contrast between this view and the European-American model of the world provides the context for much of the novel's action. As Helen Jaskoski has pointed out, *Ceremony* highlights two very different ways of understanding the world: "Native American thought . . . seeks understanding that is holistic and integrating . . . . The Western—European or Euroamerican—world view, by contrast, tends toward atomism and the disintegration of dissection and calculation."[4] White doctors have tried to cure Tayo by separating the threads. They give him "facts" about time and space—Josiah could not have been on a Pacific island; Tayo's cursing the rain in the Philippines could not affect weather thousands of miles away. When Tayo expresses concern for his people, the doctors tell him that he has to "think only of himself, and not about the others, that he would never get well as long as he used words like 'we' and 'us.'"[5] They insist that the connections he sees are illusory and that he must conceive of himself as an individual whose problems are not linked to those of the land and the people. To them, seeing connections between his actions in the Pacific, Josiah's death, and the drought is neurotic thinking which he must change. Tayo tries to believe them, but at some level he knows that "the world didn't work that way. His sickness was only part of something larger, and his cure would be found only in something great and inclusive of everything."[6]

This opposition between the "American" and Pueblo views of things is repeated at every level. Again and again we see that white culture in America works to separate things, to deny that the world is the fragile web of connections that Ku'oosh describes. White culture has its one story—the story in which the individual "succeeds" on his own by denying precisely the connections that give meaning to the American Indian world. Christianity separates the individual from the clan, "encouraging each person to stand alone, because Jesus Christ would save only the individual soul."[7] The weapons created by the whites separate the killer from his victim, so that Tayo doesn't even know whether he has killed anyone during the war. Josiah points out that scientific cattle breeding separates the cattle from the land, making them unable to live without the feed and water brought to them by humans, and leaving them "scared because the land is unfamiliar."[8]

One of the most disturbing aspects of this message is its effect on education. At schools run by whites, promising Indian children are told, "don't let the people at home hold you back,"[9] and white science teachers dismiss as "superstitions" the stories that connect the Indian children to nature. When the Navajo students are horrified by the sight of the dead frogs they are supposed to dissect in biology class, for example, the teacher laughs so hard that "he even had to wipe tears from his eyes."[10] For the Navajo children the frogs are related beings whose mistreatment will have consequences; for the white teachers they are disconnected objects of study, and dissection is a necessary rite of passage into a universe of objects. Moreover, when they attack the stories that protect frogs, the teachers destroy the children's connection not only to the natural world but to their parents and their ancestors. In a perfect illustration of Silko's view, the scalpel that severs the sinews of the frog also cuts apart a whole people and the stories that make their world.

The ability to separate things apparently gives the whites great power. Because we do not acknowledge the same kind of connection to the land, the plants, the animals, or other groups of humans, we can use them seemingly without limits, creating wealth and luxuries that earlier cultures could only dream of. The price we pay, however, is a terrible one: We also become destroyers who know and use only parts of things, cutting them away from the whole and often causing the death of what we touch. Since our science turns everything into objects separate from the beholding mind, we find ourselves cut off from and fearful of direct contact with a nature from which our stories exclude us. Finally, our power, like that of Indian witches, threatens to claim those who wield it as its ultimate victims: Those who live in desert habitats, for example, are finding out that mistreating frogs by destroying their riparian habitat does cause flood and drought, and after decades of "conquering nature," we are coming to fear destruction by the forces that we have unleashed.

Indeed, according to the Navajo shaman Betonie, Europeans were invented by Indian witches as tools who would provide the dead bodies that witchery thrives on. The most powerful of the witches creates a destructive culture by telling a story which becomes real in the telling: The people "grow away from the earth," and see a world composed of objects. The sun, the plants, the stones, the animals are "not alive" for them and "the world is a dead thing for them." The lines of Betonie's story that sum up the consequences of this view are chilling in their implications:

They fear
They fear the world.
They destroy what they fear.
They fear themselves.[11]

White culture gets its power by breaking the web of relationship and separating the individual from other beings, but the result is an emptiness which we have tried in vain to fill "with patriotic wars and with great technology and the wealth it brought."[12] Nevertheless, in this view of things, white people are not evil. The destructive aspect of our culture is simply a powerful embodiment of the urge within all humans to gain power over the world by treating it as separate and fragmented. Whites, Silko insists, become the primary victims of that power, suffering from "the dissolution of their consciousness into dead objects: the plastic and neon, the concrete and steel."[13] Believing that mountains and rivers can be owned, that animals and plants can be understood by cutting them apart, that people can be healed in isolation from each other and the land, European American culture ensures its own suffering at the hands of the witchery it serves. Similarly, the Laguna people such as Emo, Harley, and Auntie, who participate in this attempt to gain power through separation, are equally in danger of becoming witches themselves.

Completing the Ceremony

"The only cure," we are told at the beginning of the novel, "is a good ceremony"— a recognition and acting out of the connections that shape our lives. As Louis Owens has shown, it is by learning to love T'seh—a living woman who is at the same time Yellow Woman from traditional stories and the embodiment of the land itself—and by seeing "the way all the stories fit together . . . to become the story that was still being told," that Tayo is healed and "will succeed in restoring balance to his world."[14] Silko's depiction of this healing process is complex and subtle, but we can follow its progress by focusing on the scenes with Night Swan and T'seh, on the role of the speckled cattle that Josiah buys, and on the climactic scene at the Jackpile uranium mine.

Silko sets up Tayo's encounter with Night Swan by having him do a ceremony at a desert spring before he leaves for the war. This scene shows us a ceremony in its simplest form: Tayo goes to the spring at sunrise, gathers yellow flowers "the color of the sunlight," and sprinkles the pollen from the flowers onto the water.¹⁵ The rest of the ceremony is internal; Josiah has told Tayo that prayer "should be something he felt inside himself."¹⁶ Yet we can see in these few actions an embodiment of the connections that make the world what it is. Sunrise, we are told later, is "an event which in a single moment gathered all things together—the last stars, the mountaintops, the clouds, and the winds—celebrating this coming."¹⁷ The yellow flowers embody the connection between sun and earth, and sprinkling their pollen, their creative essence, on the water enacts the unity of the forces that constantly create the world—the water and sun bringing life from the soil. Having completed these simple actions, Tayo sees the world transformed before him. As each of the animals comes out—the spider, the frogs, the dragonflies—he remembers the stories associated with them and sees "a world made of stories."¹⁸

This scene is important for students' understanding of the novel, because it really demonstrates the way a ceremony works. We use symbols to act out our connection to the sacred, the powers that sustain us in the world, and in that acting out we are reminded of who we are, of the stories that place us in relationship with those powers.

The day after this ceremony, rain comes: "It was spinning out of the thunderclouds like gray spider webs and tangling against the foothills of the mountain."¹⁹ This image reminds us of Spider Woman, the creator/helper who creates and sustains the world. The rain waters the wilting crops, and it also leads to Tayo's encounter with Night Swan. If we look closely at the imagery of this encounter, we can see just how Night Swan further connects Tayo to the elements of the world. She is dressed in blue, the Pueblo color associated with rain, and her room is furnished with a blue chair and a bed covered with blue sheets. She looks ageless to Tayo "like the rain and the wind." As they come together, Silko reinforces the connection: "She moved under him, her rhythm merging into the sound of the wind shaking the rafters and the sound of the rain in the tree."²⁰

We can compare to this the imagery Silko uses to depict Tayo's encounter with T'seh after the ceremony that Betonie performs: "[H]e eased himself deeper within her and felt the warmth close around him like river sand." Moreover, the climax of their encounter is compared to a flood: "When it came, it was the edge of a steep riverbank crumbling under the downpour until suddenly it all broke loose and collapsed into itself."²¹ Clearly, these sexual encounters are to be seen as part of the process of Tayo's continuing reconnection, first with the rain and then with earth it nourishes, and they stand in sharp contrast to the sexual encounters that Emo and Harley relive in the bar scenes. In the barroom stories women are collections of parts, trophies to be displayed like the teeth from the Japanese colonel that Emo spills onto the table at the climax of the ceremony of hatred and destruction represented by the stories of the war. Tayo's sexual encounters have the opposite effect: Instead of reducing people to parts, they connect the individuals involved in a very deep way, and they also show the connection of both to the earth and the sky.

Moreover, we can see a very interesting development in Tayo's consciousness as we move from one scene to the other. In the first Tayo is "lost somewhere, deep beneath the surface of his own body and consciousness."[22] In the second, we are told that Tayo is afraid of being lost, but he follows the "trail marks" he sees in his interaction with T'seh, and "he did not get lost."[23] Each encounter comes after a ceremony (Tayo's prayer at the spring and the scalp ceremony performed by Betonie), but the language about getting lost suggests that, by the time he encounters T'seh, Tayo is more fully aware of his participation in the ceremony, better able to participate without getting lost in the moment.

Later, when T'seh comes to the ranch where Tayo is tending the speckled cattle that he has reclaimed with her help, we see the completion of his connection. He dreams that he makes love to her in the sand of a riverbed, and in the dream the distinction between her and the river sand disappears: "[H]e couldn't feel where her body ended and the sand began," and when he awakens, his fists are full of sand.[24] Shortly after this, T'seh gives Tayo the key to her identity: When he asks her name, she answers in a highly significant way: "I'm a Montaño," she said. "You can call me T'seh."[25] The Laguna name for Mount Taylor, where Tayo finds the cattle and where rain originates after the ceremony he performs before the war, is *Tse-pi'na*, Woman Veiled in Clouds. As the mountain ka'tsina, the human embodiment of the mountain's spirit, T'seh completes the process begun by Night Swan and brings Tayo back into connection with the land and the powers that bring the rain and end both the drought and his own illness.

This healing brought by T'seh corresponds with finding the speckled cattle and bringing them back to the ranch. Speckled imagery is very important in the novel, since speckledness represents a connection to the earth. We see this early in the work when Tayo rubs gypsum dust from the plaster of Night Swan's apartment on his hands the way ceremonial dancers did with white clay. As he looks at the spotted pattern the white dust makes, "he knew why it was done by the dancers; it connected them to the earth."[26] Josiah reinforces this image of connection as he discusses his plan to breed cattle that can withstand drought.

"Scientific" cattle breeding Josiah points out, separates the cattle from the land, and "they are scared because the land is unfamiliar." The speckled cattle, on the other hand, know the land and hunt water like "desert antelope."[27] The contrast between the connection to the land represented by speckling and the separation from the land valued by European culture is reinforced at the end of this discussion when Auntie, who disapproves of Josiah's plan to breed "Indian cattle," prepares for church. She very carefully examines her shoes "to make sure that any dust or spots of dirt left from last Sunday had been removed."[28] White culture respects spotlessness and the separation from the earth that comes with that kind of purity.

By finding the cattle Tayo connects himself to the land in a very practical way—they will enable him to make a living without leaving the reservation. Silko repeatedly compares the cattle to deer and antelope, the animals that enabled the Pueblo people to sustain themselves before the coming of Europeans. It is not possible to bring the game back yet, but Tayo can raise the cattle in the way Josiah envisioned and save himself from the fate of those who leave the reservation and end up in the arroyos of Gallup. After Tayo is reunited with T'seh at the ranch, he remembers watching as the bull he has borrowed from his cousin approached the speckled cattle. The bull is the color "of yellow sandrock broken loose from a cliff," and the speckled cows are like deer, "their spotted hides blending into the sandy talus of the big mesa." As Tayo watches the new calves sired by the bull, "he could see Josiah's vision emerging, he could see the story taking form in bone and muscle."[29] As Betonie has told him, the ceremonies and ways of life must change or the people will die. Tayo cannot bring back the deer and antelope that have been killed or driven away by European settlers, but he can bring to life Josiah's vision of connection, a story about living in harmony with the land, the sandrock cliffs, the sandy talus, the cycles of rain and drought.

This accomplishment of balance and connection makes Tayo a target for witchery, which works to destroy him. Emo tells the white authorities that Tayo is crazy so they will come looking for him to lock him up, and T'seh warns him to stay hidden until the Americans get tired of searching. As he hikes into the remote country far from the main roads, Tayo can feel the balance and peace of the land in a way he has not been able to before, but he is lured into taking a ride with Harley and Leroy, who claim to be cruising around aimlessly, but have been intentionally looking for him. The imagery of the ride in Harley's speeding pickup is a remarkable symbol for the effect of technology on our perception of the world around us. The enclosing glass and steel, the motion of the speeding truck, and the beer combine to separate Tayo from the land, the past, and the ceremony. The trees and hills, which only hours before had contributed to a sense of wholeness and strength, now streak by "like movie film," and the sensations of speed, enclosure, and "the warmth of beer in the belly" make the past seem "like a vague dream." He will hide here, Tayo decides, playing the role of "just . . . another drunk Indian."[30]

Students can readily identify with this tendency of technology and the speed it produces to turn the world into a movie, into something with which we have no real connection. Wrapped in glass and steel, watching the world through windows or on screens, it is easy to think that we are safe, that we are removed from the forces that are working for destruction and death. Moreover, the friendships formed within that enclosed world reinforce the patterns that keep us separated from our responsibility, our participation in the continuing creation of the trees and hills. Tayo, like us, eventually has to realize that the speeding pickup, far from keeping him safely isolated, is bearing him into the heart of witchery.

The scene that depicts his arrival there—at the Jackpile uranium mine—is the climax of the novel, and it brings all the themes and imagery together. The ore from the mine was used to build the bombs that destroyed Hiroshima and Nagasaki, and that process shows the ultimate example of witchery—the breaking apart of the atom (literally that which cannot be cut) in order to destroy and thereby gain power. In Silko's description, the uranium ore is "bright and alive as pollen," and it forms "mountain ranges and rivers across the stone." In short, it represents the potential of the earth itself, with its inherent creativity and beauty. Driven by witchery, though, those who made the bomb had "taken these beautiful rocks from deep within earth and . . . had laid them in a monstrous design, realizing destruction on a scale only *they* could have dreamed." This is witchery affecting the world at the most basic level of existence. At the same time, the scene itself brings relief to Tayo, since he can understand now why he saw Josiah's face on a Japanese soldier, why he has seen connections that others say are crazy. He understands in this moment that "human beings were one clan again, united by the fate the destroyers planned for all of them, for all living things." He also sees that he "had never been crazy. He had only seen and heard the world as it always was: no boundaries, only transitions through all distances and time."[31]

In Silko's vision of the world in *Ceremony*, we are called on, above all, to witness—to see first the beauty, connectedness, and creativity of the world and second the witchery that lies in all of us and works against that beauty and creativity. In that witnessing we help to undo the enchantment woven by those who seek power through destruction. As Tayo reflects on what is happening on this night of the autumnal equinox, he realizes that this is the night of balance, the night on which he can complete the ceremony by keeping the stories from those who would destroy them, "the last night and the last place, when the darkness of night and the light of day were balanced." The brief excerpt from the Arrowboy story that Silko includes here shows the importance of witnessing: As the witches in the story perform their rites, things go wrong and the transformation is left incomplete because Arrowboy is watching the proceedings: "Something is wrong," the witch says, "Ck'o'yo magic won't work/if someone is watching us."[32] As Robert M. Nelson has pointed out, Silko has changed things from the traditional versions of the Arrowboy story in order to emphasize the importance of vision. In those versions the failure of the transformation leads to the detection of Arrowboy, who is then forced to participate in the witchery.[33] Here Tayo is nearly tricked into becoming a participant by driving a screwdriver into Emo's skull. At the last moment, however, he understands that he would have completed the witch ceremony by accomplishing Emo's death. That act would have reaffirmed the story of Indian failure: "He would have been another victim, a drunk Indian war veteran settling an old feud." The whites would shake their heads over another Indian who could not survive in the modern world, and the Laguna people would blame themselves for not being able to save one of their own.[34]

Thus, by refusing to kill Emo, Tayo keeps the story and the ceremony intact, and the witchery, having been seen for what it is, will turn on itself, as Harley, Leroy, and Pinky are all killed and Emo moves to California. Tayo sees that "The transition was completed," and he is able to report to the elders that he has seen T'seh and that the connection to the land has been reestablished:

> They started crying
> the old men started crying
> "A'moo'ooh! A'moo'ooh!"
> You have seen her
> We will be blessed
> again.[35]

The last word in the novel—"Sunrise"—reminds us that this work is a ceremony itself. In reading it attentively we too enact the wholeness of the world and witness both the beauty of the connections and the destruction that witchery works to bring about by separating us from each other and the land.

The World of the Classroom

Now picture the world of separation and specialization into which the teacher brings this novel. The classrooms in which I teach are gray rectangles of concrete block, their space separated as carefully as possible from anything that might distract the student's attention. Their shape and arrangement proclaim the separation between the specialist and the students he or she lectures to—students sit in lines facing the front, and in order to see the faces of other students, they must struggle against the room. In addition, this classroom lies within an academic battleground on which relationship has long been losing to specialization and separation. In the last few years at the university where I teach, the College of Sciences and Humanities has been divided into three colleges, all competing with each other for resources, and a Writing Department has been extracted from the English Department. An indignant student complained to me recently because I graded her writing in a World Literature course, even though, as she protested, it was not a writing course. Despite praiseworthy efforts by organizations such as the American Culture Association, the Association for the Study of Literature and Environment, and others, most universities seem to give lip service to "interdisciplinary studies" while the disciplines in the university are actually moving away from each other faster than the galaxies in the universe.

Of course, people like me are contributing our share to the isolation. Movements in literary criticism which started out attempting to place the text in the world from which extreme versions of "New Criticism" had threatened to remove it have become so highly specialized that many of us write for tiny audiences in language that baffles and repels the uninitiated—and sometimes even the initiated: As an occasional reader for an interdisciplinary journal, I am often dismayed to receive articles in my own field that I can understand only by carefully and painstakingly translating the jargon into something like English. Pressure to publish creates "original" readings of works—often highly ingenious but idiosyncratic interpretations having little to do with the shared experience of stories. Moreover, the system does not give us time for the kind of understanding old Ku'oosh speaks of—we have to cover the period so our students will succeed on the Rising Junior Exam or the GRE.

The result of all this is that students have often been taught to approach literary works as puzzles existing in a void. I have found that many of them do not expect to understand the literal level, the story, in the works they read. Since everything in a work of literature means something else for reasons they do not quite understand, the important thing is to "interpret," i.e., discover a mysterious meaning for each part of the text without worrying too much about the story. You may have seen the humorous discussion of how to succeed at college which circulated on email a while ago, in which students are advised to approach texts in their English classes by affirming that nothing is what it seems to be. Never say that Moby-Dick is a whale, the anonymous author advises, say he's the Republic of Ireland. This line, I fear, exaggerates but captures all too well a common student perception about the mysterious way their teachers derive "meaning" from a literary work. Literary analysis seems to consist in finding an abstruse and original meaning for each part so we do not mistake the work for a story.

I cannot claim to have found a solution to all these problems, but thinking about them has, I believe, led me to some discoveries. The first is that "analysis" is an inappropriate term for what most of are trying to do as teachers and scholars. The more I reflected on my student's question about analyzing *Ceremony*, the more clearly I realized that true literary study consists not of breaking apart but of making connections. When we ask, "Why this word, this image, this metaphor?" what we mean is "How does this mean in relation to the story, to everything else in the work? What other stories does this image bring to the work, and how can we tell those so that others will see the connections?" No word or image or story can be known by itself. We are not laboratory scientists presiding over students as they learn to dissect their frogs. I think that on our best days we are more like Ku'oosh as he tells the stories about "why things must be said this certain way."

So one of our major tasks, I think, is to make this clear to students. I most often discuss *Ceremony* in a sophomore honors course on "The Cultures of America," which I team taught for many years with Patricia Washington McGraw, an African American professor who fortunately is quite willing to try new approaches. With her cooperation and help I arrived at an approach that emphasizes connections rather than parts or analysis. After spending some time introducing the novel and helping students deal with the difficult narrative voice of its opening sections, I put them in groups of three or four and tell each to begin at a designated *place* in the novel, a particularly meaningful or significant scene or episode. Their instructions are first, and primarily, to explore the place and discover how it is connected to its surroundings, to other major scenes in the book. If their scene seems particularly closely tied to that of another group, I encourage them to talk to that group. Once they have a grasp of the novel as a whole, they are asked to make connections between *Ceremony* and Native

American stories we have read earlier—a selection of creation, trickster, and hero stories from various cultures. I also ask them to think about connections to other works we have read: African and African American myths and tales, works by such European American icons as John Winthrop, Benjamin Franklin, and Thomas Jefferson, and Ralph Ellison's *Invisible Man*. Once they have finished reading the novel, they are assigned short works by such writers as Gary Soto, Amy Tan, Jimmy Santiago Baca, Michael Anthony, Barbara Kingsolver, and others, and they are asked to see how those works connect with *Ceremony*. Finally, I ask them to think about how the novel might have shed light on other courses they are taking and on their own experiences. They can present their results to the class in any way they choose, and I encourage them to think of ways that fit what they have discovered through their reading. Once they understand the task, I let them talk, simply wandering around the room to answer questions and ensure that the groups stay focused. They do. In fact, most of them take their discussions outside the classroom and spend quite a bit of time on their own, working on their understanding of the works and planning their presentations. I originally pestered the groups quite a bit, trying to ensure that they were finding what I wanted them to find. More recently, however, I have discovered that if I leave them alone their presentations are more interesting. They can find things that surprise me.

Interestingly, many of those presentations become ceremonies themselves, involving, sometimes literally, the creation of webs, the acting out of relationships among people and literary works. Students discover connections between the Cherokee story of the Bear Man and the scene in which Tayo and Rocky kill the deer. They discover witchery in Ellison's *Invisible Man*. If they are from rural areas or small towns, they find that they too have been told, "Don't let the people at home hold you back."

This does not mean, of course, that they are allowed to ignore differences between cultures. They see that the vision of *Ceremony* arises from a particular culture and that we must remember that our assumptions may differ from those of the writers and characters we study. We deal with the controversy over Silko's use of Laguna stories in ways that some Pueblo writers object to and discuss the significance of stories in that particular tradition.[36] Nevertheless, for all its particularity, *Ceremony* also becomes the center of threads that pull together the works that students have read in the course of the semester.

All this takes time: We devote at least three weeks to our discussion of *Ceremony* and are prepared to spend even more time if necessary. As Ku'oosh says, understanding the stories takes great patience and love. Once students start discovering connections, it can be hard for them to decide how to limit their presentations. Among other things they learn that any approach to a work of literature must try to limit and select in ways that do not significantly distort the whole. But by the end of the presentations the class is clearly much more closely knit and has a sense of how the whole course fits together, how all the stories are part of the same story, and how that story is the one they are living. If nothing else, I hope, *Ceremony* enables them to see that stories are central to our identity and that understanding them does not mean taking them apart or finding an interpretation that no one else is likely to arrive at. Ideally, they learn to hear the echoes and resonances among the stories and to find themselves within them.

Finally, they might also learn what Simon Ortiz tells us in his poems and essays: To understand the issues is to see the need for action, to begin to live our lives in ways that work against the destroyers and for the survival of the people and the land. The last two times I have taught the honors course, we have ended the class by cooking breakfast together during the final exam period, using ingredients that are organic and/or produced by local farmers. That way we can better understand just how to begin living the story of connection to the land.

Chapter 4

"Made of Prayers":
Luci Tapahonso and Navajo Culture

Student Misperceptions

As I suggested in the last chapter, in most of my classes I have students do reading response journals, daily writing assignments of about a page in length in which students discuss their responses to the readings and give concrete examples of the details that provoked that response. These journals can be one of the greatest burdens and greatest resources available to teachers. They are a burden because they must be read and returned immediately in order to have their greatest effect. Since our usual load is four courses per semester, I generally have to devote at least an hour or two a day to reading journals. On the other hand, there is no better way that I know of to find out what is happening as a class of students engages (or fails to engage) with the works they are reading. The journals also raise the level of discussion in the class significantly: Most students come to class having actually read and even thought about the works. I encourage students to be honest and informal, to tell me when they like the works and when they do not, on the condition that they say why and give examples. I respond to their responses, and in the best cases we have a continuing conversation that lasts all semester.

In the process of reading hundreds of these journals each semester, I have discovered something surprising and important about the way American Indian literature is often taught, or at least about the message many students think they have been given by their teachers: American Indian writers, in their minds, are victims trying to provoke guilt in the reader. I probably should not have been too surprised to discover this, given that such readings as "surrender speeches," the sentimental "Chief Seattle's Reply," and other works of rather dubious authority are often presented as an introduction to American Indian literature and culture. Nevertheless, it came as quite a shock to me that students would have a perception so completely different from the reality I had experienced in my reading and my interactions with American Indian people. The student response to this way of presenting American Indians is often hostility. As Herman Melville's narrator says in "Bartleby the Scrivener," "To a sensitive being, pity is not seldom pain. And when at last it is perceived that such pity cannot lead to effectual succor, common sense bids the soul be rid of it."[1] Though they do not express it quite so elegantly, my students often feel the same way. Recently, in fact, a graduate student who is studying to be a teacher wondered in her journal how she could keep high school students from feeling that *Ceremony* is specifically designed to produce guilt in the white reader. She was afraid that the opening poem, with its declaration that "they" try to destroy the stories, would feel like an accusing finger pointed at the reader. I am always careful to point out that the "they" in that poem refers to witches, not specifically to white people, but the future high school teacher's point is a valid one: Students feel helpless in the face of injustices that happened many years ago, so they become resentful when such abuses are presented as the main focus of American Indian literature. The obverse of this is almost as bad—a settled guilt that also leads students to see only accusation and to overlook everything else. Both attitudes keep students from seeing what is really there in the literature. When we are defensive we interpret everything as attack, and when we feel that we have guilt to expiate we can overlook the strengths, adaptations, and wisdom of the cultures we think we have "destroyed."

American Indian literature does, of course, point out injustice and abuse, but the focus is quite different from what my students perceive. As Leslie Marmon Silko reminds us in *Ceremony*, we as European Americans must understand our culture's role in the injustices that have happened, not because American Indians want us to feel guilty, but because otherwise we will fail to see that they have happened and are happening to us too. Only then will we understand with Tayo that "human beings [are] one clan," united in our vulnerability to the witchery that turns all beings into objects to be manipulated.[2] On our first trip to the Southwest, a student asked Ray Coin, our Hopi guide, what one thing he most wanted us to take with us from our visit. He didn't hesitate: "The knowledge that we're all one people," he said. The Hopi do their ceremonies for all beings, he added, because all of us make mistakes and need healing. That is what the stories teach. Diane Glancy makes a similar point in the poem cited in the first chapter of this book. As she reflects on "another semester" of teaching American Indian literature and culture, she asks herself just what her class has to offer the students. After a list of possible lessons, she concludes that the study of American Indian literature and culture finally gives you "the core of yourself/you carry with you wherever you go."[3] This opportunity to learn about ourselves and our connections to others is precisely what can be overlooked if we see American Indians as victims.

Navajo tradition adds to this more complex picture an amazing adaptive ability. Far from rejecting all aspects of European culture, the Navajo have incorporated horses, sheep, goats, silverwork, the weaving of woolen blankets and rugs, and other European innovations into their culture, not through imitation or assimilation, but by really transforming these raw materials into parts of a dynamic tradition that is always changing yet always remains Navajo. They embody one of the things Glancy's poem says American Indian cultures can teach us: "It's transformation which is the constant."[4] Like the church at Acoma that I described in the first chapter, Navajo tradition grows and thrives by incorporating other stories into its own.

In my experience, Luci Tapahonso's poems and stories offer an excellent antidote to the perception that American Indian peoples see themselves as victims. More than any other author included in this book, she gives us the everyday life of a traditional American Indian people as they live in and cope with "America." The world of the Navajo (or Diné) comes across in her pages as a complex and usually joyful place where past injustices and present tragedies are remembered and noted, but life is lived with a deep appreciation, not only for the ancient traditions that provide the foundation for life, but for the way life is now. To be sure, there is sadness in many of her stories. Living in Kansas, for example, she laments the need to leave the people and land of Dinetah to return to her teaching duties, an inevitable sacrifice for one who wants to survive as a poet in America, but one that is especially difficult for a traditional Navajo. In "The Weekend Is Over," as she and her daughters get ready to begin the drive from Shiprock, New Mexico, to Lawrence, she sums up the pain she feels at having to leave the community that is Dinetah: "My throat is so heavy, I can hardly swallow."[5] In another example of sadness explored, she retells the story of the "Long Walk" in her poem "In 1864," and describes the "tears [that] stream down" her daughter's face as the story is concluded.[6] But sadness is always balanced in her poems by a sense of life to be lived: As "The Weekend is Over" concludes, she begins the trip back to Kansas not only with memories of family smiles but also with "coffee brewed over an open fire/and mutton and green chile wrapped in warm tortillas for all of us."[7] For her, Navajo life includes the coffee, mutton, and wheat brought by the Spanish as well as the green chiles and open fires of traditional Navajo culture, and, though she must be separated from family for a time, she can take the smiles and warm tortillas with her. As we will see below, she concludes her story of the "Long Walk" in a similar way.

Moreover, Tapahonso often writes with an engaging sense of humor, a quality that she identifies as an important part of Navajo culture. She can confess that she dresses up whenever an airline flight takes her through Texas because a friend of hers saw George Strait in the Dallas/Fort Worth Airport. "[T]he world is basically good," she says, "and so I am certain that one day/ I will just happen to run into George Strait in Texas."[8] She can tell humorous and richly detailed stories about recovering a stolen dog that has been taken to a remote part of the reservation, only to discover days later that the "recovered" dog does not have the cropped ears, bobbed tail, or even the same sex of the original.[9] She tells about jumping from her friend's beloved Kharman-Ghia while it is still rolling because the cute car her friend just had to buy does not have brakes.[10] Poems and stories such as these can give students a way into her world, and they can completely undercut their expectations that American Indian literature will be about unrelieved tragedy and victimhood. Indeed, some of my rural students identify with the long series of goodbyes in "The Weekend Is Over." That is what happens when they go home, too.

In her richest work, then, Tapahonso brings together history and traditions from the past with the richness she finds in life in the present. While these encounters nearly always include tension and sadness, they are generally life affirming, not out of shallow optimism, but because the Navajo view of life makes that sadness into part of what gives the present its richness, and because the Navajo emphasis on adaptation without assimilation (what is sometimes called "survivance") provides an inherently flexible and creative approach to life, an approach that has much we can learn from. In this chapter, then, I will look at four poems from two different collections that show this approach to literature and that can be used to give students a more accurate view of just what American Indian literature is about.

"In 1864"

The poem "In 1864," mentioned earlier, is perhaps a good place to start seeing just how Tapahonso manages this balance of sadness and affirmation. After an epigraph briefly describing the Navajo "Long Walk," the poem opens in the present with a mother and daughter making a car trip to Fort Sumner, the location of the "Bosque Redondo" where Navajo people were taken after being captured or starved into surrender by the army. However, instead of immediately recounting the events of 1864, Tapahonso tells of another more recent journey, that of a Navajo man who goes to Fort Sumner to work as an electrician installing power lines. After three nights the man has to leave. He tells his co-workers that it is because he misses his family, but the real reason is the cries and moans he hears around his trailer each night. "The place contained the pain and cries of his relatives,/the confused and battered spirits of his own existence."[11] The second line here is particularly important in understanding the rest of the poem because it reveals a way of seeing that is quite different from the European American view. The cries are not just those of relatives who died long ago; they are cries of the man's own spirit, since in Navajo tradition the lives, the suffering and joys, of relatives are very much a part of the present. As Tapahonso points out in an interview with Andrea Penner, she and the other Navajo poets in an anthology Tapahonso has edited are distinguished from European Americans and even in some ways from other American Indian peoples by "a real strong emphasis on heritage": "They are conscious of kinship; they are different in that way."[12] Navajos living today remember that they are who they are because their ancestors worked and suffered and prayed. There is no boundary between relatives, between those who lived in the past and those who live now. Indeed, the actual story of the Long Walk begins with the speaker's aunt's reminder: "'You are here/because of what happened to your great grandmother long ago.'"[13]

Before that story begins, however, we are brought back into the present with a stop for "Coke and chips." This use of time is very important to the movement of the poem: It brings us back in an interesting way into a world in which the speaker and her daughter participate in American culture as it is, and thus it serves to remind us of the life that continues in spite of changes and the suffering the poem will describe so vividly.

The description of the Long Walk itself gains a personal dimension from the voice of the aunt reminding the listener of its significance, yet it is ultimately told in the voice of yet another person, an unnamed speaker who actually participated in the events. This overlay of voices—a speaker who tells the story in the voice of the aunt, who tells it in the voice of an earlier ancestor—reinforces our sense of the way in which the past forms the present. There can be no single voice, because every voice contains the voices of those who have made this speaking possible.

The story itself pulls no punches. When the American soldiers are able to kill the people's sheep in front of them, the speaker says, "It was then I knew our lives were in great danger."[14] Men who could heartlessly kill the sheep who were like family to the Navajo must be capable of anything. Once again, the story highlights the importance and extended meaning of family and stresses the destructive nature of a perspective that can so easily ignore family bonds. The details of the journey itself are familiar to anyone who has studied the history of the Navajo, but once again they are given power through the voice of the teller as she records her response to the events. The speaker's "heart hurts" as she remembers the old people who could not keep up and were abandoned, the pregnant women taken behind a rock and shot, the children and older men who drowned trying to cross the flood-swollen Rio Grande. The voice tells us, "We must never forget their screams and the last we saw of them."[15]

The people survived, the voice continues, because of their ability to stay together and because of the stories from the holy people. The telling of the long walk apparently returns again to the voice of the aunt, reminding the listener: "'This is why we are here.'"[16] However, the speaker of those words is referred to only as "she," leaving a purposeful ambiguity about the actual speaker. The voice of the aunt is the voice of the women who suffered and died and survived and returned, and that is the many-layered voice of the poem as well; its modern-day speaker who travels by car the route her ancestors traveled on foot also lives the story they lived within a modern setting that includes stops for Coke and chips.

The last section of the poem is the one that addresses most directly my students' misperceptions. It returns us to the present, where the speaker sees her daughter "crying softly," unable to speak. A more sentimental poet might have ended the poem here, and it would certainly have a powerful effect of a kind. Tapahonso, however, continues the story in a way that is more in keeping with the Navajo view of the world: At Bosque Redondo the people learned to use flour and to make the fry bread that is now part of Navajo culture; they learned to appreciate strong coffee and to dress in calico and velvet decorated with silver coins. The last lines offer a vivid image of Navajo vitality:

> It is always something to see–silver flashing in the sun
> against dark velvet and black, black hair.[17]

These closing lines are wonderfully evocative and dense. The flashing silver against the dark velvet vividly suggests the way in which Navajo traditions encompass both the dark and the light, the suffering of the past and the ability to transform that suffering into present joy without forgetting its significance. The ones who fell and died on the way to *Hwééldi* (the Navajo name for Bosque Redondo) still live in the mother and daughter who drive to Fort Sumner and stop along the way for Coke and chips, and their presence, for all the sadness it may provoke, is also the basis of present joy, the flash of silver. The past will be remembered, not in order to remind the Navajo that they are victims, but to communicate the spirit of the ones who died, the ones who survived, the ones who kept the old stories holy and told the new ones. The layered voice of the poem tells the people that the ancestors live not just in the original Navajo traditions but also in the fry bread and calico dresses, the coffee and velvet shirts flashing with silver coins that give beauty to Navajo life today. In the words of the ambiguous and inclusive "she," "This is why we are here./Because our grandparents prayed and grieved for us.'"[18]

This emphasis on a past that in spite of sadness and suffering gives beauty to the present is reinforced by my own interactions with Navajo people. When the members of my travel courses meet with Sunny Dooley, a Navajo storyteller from Vanderwagen, New Mexico, she often begins her discussion of Navajo culture with the story of two of her ancestors, who survived the Long Walk and Mexican slavery. The two met as her long-ago grandfather was hiding in a hollow log after escaping from soldiers in Canyon De Chelly and the girl who was escaping from slavery chose to hide in the same log as she fled from the household in Mexico where she and her sisters had been held. Sunny describes the traditional belt—carefully preserved—that her grandmother of long ago hid food in as she prepared to leave her sisters and flee north. She does not minimize the suffering and sadness of the events, the trauma of having to follow goats up the side of Canyon De Chelly to escape the soldiers as families were killed or captured below, the sadness of leaving behind the two sisters who could not hope to escape. At the same time, Sunny reminds us that she comes from that moment and that place, and that her Navajo traditions give her a beautiful and joyful way to live in this world. She wants us to leave her talk impressed by the deep spirituality and beauty of the hogan, the baskets, the dresses, and the sacred mountains that are reflected in nearly everything the Navajo make. She would agree with Tapahonso's statement in the interview with Penner that Navajos live by constant prayer; not prayers of lamentation but prayers of gratitude that constantly remind them of their connection to the Holy People who give them strength and beauty.[19]

"A Birthday Poem"

This connection with the Holy Ones is the topic of another Tapahonso poem, "A Birthday Poem," which, like "The Weekend Is Over," deals with the poet's separation from Dinetah. The poem, a remarkable example of the sestina form, opens with a beautiful image:

> This morning the sunrise is a brilliant song
> cradling tiny birds and brittle leaves.

As the speaker reminds us shortly, the white light of Dawn, like all the major elements of the Navajo world, is Diyin Din'é, that is, it is animated by one of the Holy People to whom the Navajo pray for Hózhó, "the beauty of all things being right and proper as in songs/the Holy Ones gave us."[20] Thus, morning sunshine is not just light but song, the voice of the Holy One, establishing harmony in the world. The alliterative "tiny birds and brittle leaves" reminds us of the cycle of seasons and the universality of the things the light "cradles" and nurtures, the young birds beginning life and the dry leaves signaling its end. As she faces the east to pray in the Navajo way, the speaker embodies the ceremonies, the "precise prayers" that enable humans to participate in the ongoing song of Hózhó. This ceremony from the past creates the present moment, even though the speaker is far away from Dinetah. She asks for the humor that Navajo elders value, the "jokes, stories, and laughter" that are also central to Hózhó. She wants to understand that the "soft hills, plains and winds" of Kansas are also Diyin, even as she plans her next trip to New Mexico.[21]

As the speaker describes that planned trip, her verb tense switches from future to present to past. When we reach the last stanzas of the poem, the trip has apparently been completed "in the tradition of Diné/travel," with laughter and singing and the appearance of Hózhó in the light of the moon over Texas, as well such seemingly mundane activities as eating and refueling. The trip completed, we find ourselves, at least in spirit, at a Night Way ceremony, where the speaker answers her daughter's questions about the Holy Ones. As she does in "In 1864," Tapahonso uses time in the poem to remind us that distinctions between past and present are arbitrary. Just as the struggles of women in 1864 inform the life of the modern speaker, the Night Way is not something that happened in a past or will happen in a future: Those who come to the ceremony "listen and absorb the songs/until they live within," giving the people their ability to "restore Hózhó, Hózhó, Hózhó, Hózhó." The repetition of the term four times (the sacred number for the Navajo) reminds us that the poem is itself a ceremony which restores harmony and balance in the speaker's world and in the world at large, even as it describes the speaker's everyday experiences in this world.

The poem ends where it begins, with a morning prayer that reminds us that we are reborn into the world and participate in the restoration of Hózhó each dawn, in spite of the ways in which "the world may overwhelm us."[22] Thus, the title, "A Birthday Poem," which makes us expect references to one person's birthday, tells us instead of the rebirth of the world and its people in the song of the dawn. "[W]e Diné," the speaker says, "are made of prayers," and that making is continuous.[23] At the same time, the poem is a birthday gift, perhaps to the daughter mentioned in the poem, but certainly to us who read it and are reminded of our participation in the constant creation of the world and ourselves.

Finally, as a sestina, the poem underscores the Navajo ability to adapt ideas and forms from other cultures to fit their own. Tapahonso uses the repetition that the sestina demands to give the poem the feeling and in some ways the effect of a ceremony. The repetition of key words—song, world, Diyin, prayers, Diné, Hózhó—effectively underscores the Navajo approach to reality and in a sense creates that world through language just as a ceremony does. Thus the challenging European form becomes an appropriate vehicle for a view of the world and of language that is distinctly Navajo.

"Starlore"

The restorative power of ceremony is explored again in "Starlore," which is a combination of prose and poetry, a combination that reminds us once again of the ways in which American Indian writers use European forms but adapt them to their own purposes. The poem begins with two paragraphs of prose: The first describes the challenges of modern life, and the second chronicles the gathering of the speaker's family and the preparation for a ceremony. "No one could have told me," the speaker says in the first sentence, "that growing older could have been this way." She goes on to list the ways in which modern life threatens the family, and yet we can see that in a way there is opportunity as well as tragedy in the examples she gives: not only children disappearing into cities and families splitting up because of "one sentence spoken in anger," but also families being tested because children go with friends to "Europe or New York." She reminds us that even "success" by European American standards— the ability to travel or go to college—challenges crucial family bonds in Navajo culture. Moreover, the Navajo students who make it to college might be "one of five Indian students," and their parents would not be able to "know all they endured."[24] Leaving the reservation means entering a world of misunderstanding and isolation.

However, in the face of this painful change, the speaker concludes, Navajo people have unchanging ways of addressing their fears. The second paragraph describes the speaker's family meeting at their parents' home to drive across the desert and gather at the home of the singer, "the one who knows the precise songs, the long, rhythmic prayers that will restore the world for us."[25] The family, having entered the hooghan in the traditional clockwise manner, waits in the sacred space, listening to the wind that offers the promise of renewing rain, ready for the ceremony that will bring them once again into Hózhó, into harmony and balance with each other and a changing world.

The speaker does not describe the ceremony itself. As Tapahonso tells Andrea Penner, she can only write about the "surface" of a ceremony. "I would never take a creation story and rewrite it or retell it," she says; "I don't think it's my place to do that."[26] The ceremony can be known in writing only by its effect, but it is nevertheless at the center of the poem. Though it is not described, it is present in what the participants feel and do afterwards. At this point Tapahonso switches to poetry, the words italicized. The changes in arrangement and typeface reinforce the change in the participants' mental and spiritual state. After the ceremony, the mundane world of prose has become the more intensely ordered world of poetry, in which each word and each relationship between words has a heightened significance.

The singer leads the people outside where they watch as *"a single star shatters"* yet remains *"whole and glowing."* *"'This,'"* the singer says, *"'has happened for all of you.'"*[27] His meaning is elaborated through the images in the next section of the poem, which describe a natural setting laden with the signs of renewing water: *"billowing rain clouds"* pass before the moon, and the people hear the sound of the river and smell *"the damp riverbank/and sweet approaching rain."*[28] The imagery shows the paradoxical but harmonious relationship between change and permanence. The star can shatter and yet remain whole; the clouds and the river are in motion, constantly changing and bringing change to the rocks that tumble in the current, yet the coming of the rain itself shows the presence of a renewal that is ancient and continuing.

The speaker takes away from the ceremony the knowledge that she is valued by the Holy Ones, *"pitied by the huge sky/the bright moon, and glittering stars."* The last lines of the poem are intensely evocative: *"I have seen the stars separate./And I am, I am."*[29] The speaker knows of her own existence because it has been shown to be inseparable from that of the stars, the clouds, the rain, and the songs that bring all this together. The Navajo know that they are made of *"prayers that have no end,"* prayers that are inseparable from the songs of the stars and the rain. To be is to know oneself in these songs. That knowledge puts even painful change into perspective: Like the stars that can shatter and remain whole, the people will continue to be in spite of the shattering, the separation and isolation, that modern life can bring. Their ancient way of living is at the same time a way that is constantly renewed, and they can draw on it in order to deal with the changes and challenges brought by the present. This is the polar opposite from the usual stereotype of victims clinging to a beautiful but outmoded way of life.

"This Is How They Were Placed for Us"

My personal favorite among Tapahonso's poems is her celebration of the sacred peaks that the Navajo see as defining their world. Written in a combination of Navajo and English, the poem declares its rootedness in Navajo tradition in the first line, which places the European American reader in the unfamiliar position of having to deal with something completely unfamiliar. A week or so before I took students to the Southwest in 2002, a Navajo friend of my sister's, blessed with great patience, generosity, and a genuine Navajo sense of humor, coached me on the meaning and pronunciation of the Navajo lines, and one of the highlights of the trip since then has been the reading and discussion of this poem as we sit in the shadow of Dook'o'oosłíí́d (the San Francisco peaks), having watched the sun rise over the shoulder of Tsoodził (Mount Taylor) a few days before, and having hiked into Canyon De Chelly with a Navajo guide and met Sunny Dooley on the rim of the canyon. When students can actually see the mountains, their understanding of the poem deepens immensely, but the poem also works well in more conventional classes to give students a deeper understanding of Navajo culture and the poet's approach to the world.

First, the use of the Navajo language is central to the poem. Though it presents difficulties for students and teachers alike (in spite of my coaching on reading this poem, I don't presume to be any kind of authority on Navajo and have to screw up my courage each time I present it), that difficulty itself represents a major value of the poem. It reminds us of what we too often forget: that there are people in this country who speak languages that are not closely related to ours. For them, English is just as much a shock as the Navajo words are to us, but they are seen as backward or stubborn if they cannot speak our language. Moreover, their cultures and their languages are inseparable. Wherever we go on the reservations in the Southwest, we hear concerns about keeping the language alive, teaching it to the children, and using it to reinforce bonds between generations that will otherwise break because of an inability to communicate on a deep level. Insofar as American culture encourages the learning of English at the expense of these languages, the process of cultural destruction continues. By insisting on the validity, and, indeed, the necessity of the Navajo language in her poem, Tapahonso is embodying the Navajo tradition of adaptation without assimilation, using a European art form (poetry) but in a way that keeps alive her people's traditions. Similarly, when Sunny Dooley comes to our campus to tell stories, she insists on using a combination of Navajo and English, so students can hear the beauty of the language and remember that it is ultimately inseparable from the stories that tell the people what they need to know.

Though Tapahonso translates most of the Navajo sentences, she sometimes places the translation where its relationship to the Navajo phrasing is not obvious. For example, in the first stanza, the English line that most closely approximates the Navajo opening is line four: "[Blanca Peak] watches us rise at dawn." Moreover, she also leaves some important phrases untranslated, most notably the phrase that serves as a refrain in each section—"bik'egho hózhónígo naashá" (because of this I walk in hózhó). This insistence on having the Navajo lines stand on their own in several places is a way of showing ownership of the poem, so to speak, of insisting that the poem is not written simply to serve an English-speaking audience but to include the speaker's native language and audience and to give them authority. It reminds us that we can participate in the poem but cannot completely understand it as outsiders. To come fully within the world of the sacred peaks will take effort on our part, a willingness to grapple with the unfamiliar and give up our assumption that we live in a country where English always plays the authoritative role. This subversion of our linguistic expectations stands for a larger subversion of cultural assumptions. Just as we must encounter a different language, we must also encounter a different cultural perspective in general.

This new cultural perspective appears immediately in the first stanza, in the line, "She watches us rise at dawn." The mountain, Blanca Peak, is not an "it." She is a person and more than a person: "the brightness of spring" and "Changing Woman returned." Both are associated with life-renewing powers, Changing Woman representing the earth's capacity to create, sustain, and renew life. As the wife of the Sun and the mother of Monster Slayer, she plays a central role in Navajo mythology and enables the people to survive and adapt.[30] The influence of this mountain is seen in the Navajo people's creative abilities, their songs and weaving, their stories and laughter, and their willingness to "believe in old values and new ideas."[31] That all this is "because of her," is repeated four times in the third stanza, signaling once again that we are in a ceremonial space. The poem is also an ordering of the world according to hózhó. The non-Navajo reader must be ready to enter a place where people are instructed by the land that surrounds them, where during each part of the day humans look to the corresponding mountain to remember what they should do to live in harmony and balance.

The following sections of the poem follow a similar pattern: each of the first four mountains represents a direction, a time of day, an activity, and a time of life with its particular values and growth. To the south Tsoo dził, or Mount Taylor, shines in the "midday sunlight" and tells her children to eat. She represents adolescence and teaches the people "to believe in all ways of learning."[32] Dook'o'oosłííd (the San Francisco peaks), embodies the West—the evening or autumn of the day, the year, and our lives, the time when we will be called "woman" or "man." Her particular teaching is the belief in strong families and the value of relatives, which, as we have seen, are central to the Navajo way of seeing the world. Finally, Dibé Nitsaa or Hesperus Peak to the north is the mountain of rest and renewal, the mountain of the night and winter in which we are called "elderly woman" or "elderly man" and will be appreciated as we enter our time of rest. She also teaches "hope for good things,"[33] giving a sense that night and winter are not to be feared but are to be embraced as both the time of rest and the time of looking forward to the mystery that the cycles of the day, the year, and our lives reveal. Within the circle defined by the peaks sit the fifth and sixth mountains, Huerfano Mountain and Gobernador Knob, dressed in "precious fabrics" and "sacred jewels." The description of Gobernador Knob can stand here as representative of the imagery that gives the poem its incredible beauty:

> Gobernador Knob is clothed in sacred jewels.
> She wears mornings of white shell.
> She wears the midday light of turquoise.
> She wears evenings of abalone, the light of the moon.
> She wears nights of black jet.[34]

Having grown up in Tucson, at the feet of the Santa Catalina Mountains to the east and the Tucson range to the west, I cannot think of a more evocative description of the mysterious beauty of mountains as they go through the changes each day brings. This last mountain becomes the summing up of the others, and by extension the embodiment of all mountains. Within the poem, this description functions as a kind of distillation: as we read of the white shell, turquoise, abalone, and jet, each of which is associated with its own mountain, we understand that those "sacred jewels" have meanings far beyond any we could have imagined before reading the poem. They give us the beauty of mountains changing as the day passes, but they also remind us of the beauty of change in our lives, of the values that the land teaches, and of a constant connection to wisdom that is there in the land itself to be seen at each time of the day with its changing light and its movement through the seasons.

The last stanzas focus on the seventh presence within the circle of the six mountains: the people themselves as they affirm their existence in and through the sacred place, dressing as they are taught to by the mountains, living by the truths the mountains teach, valuing both old ways and new ideas, growing strong and prosperous with the strength and values of the land, which include accepting and even thriving on the changes that are embodied in the land with its seasons of the day and year. The last line, "This is where our prayers began," reminds us once again that the Navajo are a people made of prayer, prayer that is their part in the song that the holy beings are singing during every hour of each day.

"Made of Prayers"

Luci Tapahonso's Poetry in the Classroom

As another Southwestern poet from a different tradition, Alberto Rios, reminds us, "Words are our weakest hold on the world."[35] Each time I prepare to teach this poem, I nearly despair of being able to find the words that might communicate its beauty and wisdom to students who live in such a different cultural world. It is only when I know that I will have the help of the San Francisco Peaks, the more talented teacher Dook'o'oosłííd, standing over my shoulder that I can feel relatively comfortable about leading a student discussion. The lines of this poem evoke feelings in me and, I believe, in students who read it carefully and with some humility, that words of explanation cannot fully describe. Even as we struggle with its unfamiliar language, its different cultural assumptions, and its surprising imagery, however, we are drawn into a beautiful place, a world in which the land is intensely alive and beautiful and the people know they are alive and beautiful through that life.

As Simon Ortiz tells us, the truth that the people are the land is not culturally determined or even metaphorical. As modern Americans we may draw our being in part from places we have never seen, the soil of New Zealand in the form of apples or the land of China or Indonesia in our shoes or shirts, but we are the land. We are the soil and the air and the clouds and the mountains in our own peculiarly animated embodiment. The land forms us and teaches us and gives us whatever strength we have. Luci Tapahonso and her Navajo traditions understand this. Far from defining themselves as victims waiting for "America" to repent of its sins and fix their lives, they offer us a glimpse of a life lived in awareness of this vital truth, a life made of prayer.

As European Americans, we have to acknowledge the guilt and injustice that are part of our heritage. That is probably true of every other people as well, though in the case of European cultures including ours, the list seems to be a particularly long one. We need to confront that list in order to know who we are. As European Americans, our complacency about our own history and way of life is a frustrating and dangerous characteristic that has astonished even European observers of our culture.[36] Historically we have tended to resent vehemently any suggestion that our national behavior suggests flaws in our vision. At the same time, as I have mentioned above, it is easy for us to adopt the obverse attitude and become Jeremiahs, proclaiming our guilt and the imminent destruction of Jerusalem. Both attitudes, perhaps, arise from the same source, our belief in our own chosenness. From the time of our founding, we have tended to see ourselves in the light of American historical exclusionism, the belief that we alone of all nations have a special and sacred history. There are both Christian and capitalist (and capitalist Christian) versions of this attitude, and both declare that God or history will reward us or punish our actions in ways that do not apply to other nations. That belief can make us overlook the beauty and validity in other views of the world, but it is perhaps even more dangerous when it leads us to believe that the people we have exploited and mistreated need to be brought within the embrace of "America" so we can make up for past sins. Indeed, it is not a large step from the idea that Indians are victims to the idea that we need to fix their lives for the sake of our own souls or the national conscience. As Leslie Marmon Silko suggests in *Ceremony*, some of the worst damage to American Indian people was inflicted by "holy missionary white people who... dedicated their lives to helping the Indians."[37]

A poem like "In 1864" can inject a little humility into the discussion. Yes, our government, at the urging of ordinary people who wanted a little more comfort, a little more money, a little more land, a little better sense of security—people, in short, like me, and perhaps like you—did terrible things to the Navajo. What the aunt in the poem says of her Navajo ancestors must also be said of ours: We are here because they acted as they did. It is crucial that we understand that: That capacity for violence is still in us, as our recent history has reaffirmed. It also lives in others who will respond to our violence with violence of their own. Until we can confront our capacity for injustice, the witchery that lives not just in us but in all humans, we will continue to act in ways that create suffering among other peoples, as well as in ourselves.

At the same time, we did not succeed in "victimizing" the Navajo. Students can learn by reading these poems that for Tapahonso life is beautiful and holy. There is room for humor, for a glimpse of George Strait in the Dallas airport, for the silver that flashes in the sunlight as well as the memory of ancestors who suffered and died along the way. Her people's traditions, founded in an acceptance of both change and continuity, still give them a beautiful way of living in the world. Like the star in "Starlore," they can shatter and remain whole. They can offer us the example of a truly religious life in which every moment is made by the singing of the Holy Ones, a world in which our awareness can make that song our own, even as we deal with changes that seem to threaten our traditional values. As we see in "This Is How They Were Placed for Us," the Navajo people live in a beauty taught by the land and made possible by their relatives, past and present. Speaking from that place, Luci Tapahonso no doubt wants the Navajo people to be able to determine their own future without having it "fixed" for them by Christian or capitalist missionaries, and she wants us to appreciate what can be learned from the land, but she is not particularly concerned about how "America" comes to terms with its past. That is our cross to bear.

Chapter 5

The Quiet People:
George Webb's *A Pima Remembers* and the Akimel O'odham

Creation without Conflict

My students often find the Pima creation story (as published in the Norton anthology) to be surprising in its approach to conflict. The primary creator, Juhwertamahkai, makes the world from the "greasy earth" on his breast, and when white ants have enlarged it so that he can stand on it, he creates, from "the shadow of his eye," a helper, the Buzzard Noo-ee.[1] Noo-ee, however, chooses not to help. Instead of bringing down retribution, which we might expect from our familiarity with Greek or Christian myth, Noo-ee's lack of cooperation is simply ignored. A similar situation emerges when Ee-ee-toy (also known as See-ur-huh, or "older brother") appears and claims to be older than both Juhwertamahkai and Toe-hahvs, or coyote. They argue with him for a time, but finally, "just to please him," they go along with his wish to be called older brother.[2] Later the pattern is repeated twice. We are told that Juhwertamahkai, "though really the strongest, was generous and from kindness and for relationship sake, let Ee-ee-toy have the best of it."[3] This propensity to value kindness, generosity, and peaceful relationships over "winning" is remarked on by other Pima writers. Anna Moore Shaw, for example, attributes the following words to her husband: "The white man says we Indians are not a competitive race. Well I guess they are right and I am glad of it!"[4]

My own experience with the Pima men with whom I worked construction many years ago confirms this cultural tendency to defuse tension and conflict. The Pima workers approached every situation with a humor and humility that made them a pleasure to work with. When I joined them for a poker game after work, I was intrigued to find that they had changed the rules in a very telling way: Each hand was simply played out for the original ante. There was no betting to draw cards, no raising, no bluffing. In short, there was none of the competitive tension that typical poker players value. The game was relaxed rather than dramatic; it involved playing out the cards we drew without trying to fool or intimidate the other players. I think that poker game might stand for an important tendency in Pima culture: Like Juhwertamahkai, Pima culture puts much more emphasis on harmony than on "winning."

A Pima Remembers, George Webb's combination of autobiography, cultural description, Pima stories, and gentle protest, underscores this cultural tendency. The book's longevity—it was first published in 1959 and is still in print—is a testament to its strengths, and it was included in a 1981 list by *Los Angeles Times* writer Kenneth Funsten as one of the "100 Books for the Modern Person," along with titles by writers ranging from Kenneth Galbraith and Herbert Marcuse to Ralph Ellison and Harold Bloom.[5] Despite this kind of recognition, its relative obscurity (typing "George Webb" into the MLA International Bibliography yields not a single entry, and "Pima and Literature" sends you only to an essay on Webb's unpublished novel, *Naco*) underscores an important point about the people it describes: Even in a time when significant attention is being paid to American Indian cultures and literatures, the Akimel O'odham (or Pima) often get overlooked. Though the Pima have persisted in spite of difficult circumstances and can point to a number of striking accomplishments—including one of the largest and most successful farming operations in southern Arizona and their remarkable participation in the most important study of diabetes ever undertaken—they tend to be quiet and unassuming about both their problems and their successes. It is significant that in their creation story, the Pima depict themselves as being the last people to speak, after other groups such as the Apache and the Maricopa have already begun to vocalize. Emphasizing creativity, adaptation, humility, and flexibility over self-assertion and aggressiveness, Pima culture has managed to survive and in some ways even thrive in the face of cultural conflict with its quiet response to the world, though the Pima people have also suffered from their accommodating approach to European-American culture. *A Pima Remembers* highlights both sides of that experience in ways that can engage and yet challenge students. In this chapter, then, I will use Webb's book as a way into Pima culture in general, suggesting that the Pima view of the world should be better understood as a creative and largely successful approach to maintaining traditional values in an often hostile environment. I think focusing on the Pima people might also help students to see an important point–American Indian cultures are still here, still struggling in the face of intense pressure, yet still finding ways to adapt and embody traditional values.

Good Neighbors, Not "Good Traders"

Webb begins with the deceptively simple story of a Pima family—his own ancestors—living before the appearance of European settlers. His prose style fits the purpose he declares in his preface: "This writing is done in a very simple way so that the Indian with the least education may read and understand it."[6] Ironically, this seemingly simple style is one of the greatest obstacles for university students (and perhaps for scholars as well). Many of the students I have taught have written in their journals that they had a hard time taking the work seriously: At first it seems to have been written exclusively for children. If they pay attention, however, they find a rhetorical subtlety, a quiet use of irony and humor, that rewards careful reading. Webb's subtlety, in fact, probably had a lot to do with the existence of the book, because the circumstances of publication are relatively unusual for the conservative 1950s. This is a book written by an American Indian expressly for American Indian readers, with a clear message of protest, yet it was published by a major university press, clearly an indication of Webb's diplomacy and his ability to relate skillfully to his European American neighbors.

As he describes the activities, tools, and housing of the Pima family, Webb often uses terms such as "primitive," or "crude," adjectives that may make us flinch a bit as twenty-first century readers. The overall thrust of the descriptions has quite a different effect, though: Having successfully incorporated the cattle and horses brought by the Spanish into their traditional farming and hunting activities, the Pima people Webb describes live comfortably and prosperously. They are capable warriors when the need arises—the story of Pima villagers rushing to help their Maricopa (or Pee-Posh) friends by routing a party of Yuma warriors makes that point very effectively. However, they are much more comfortable in the role of generous neighbor to the other peoples they encounter. Webb describes the interaction between his people and their Tohono O'odham cousins (formerly known as the Papago) in a typically engaging way. When they bring salt from the Gulf of California to trade for the corn and beans that the Pima have in abundance, Webb says, the Tohono feel as if they are getting the better part of the bargain, so they stay to help the Pimas harvest their wheat. The description of the two peoples working together gives a clear sense of harmony and quiet prosperity shared with others.

Even the Apaches, traditional enemies of the Pimas, are treated with generosity in Webb's narrative. He broaches the topic of the Apache raids by pointing out that the Pimas were always prosperous, but "the poor Apaches who lived in the mountains to the north did not do any farming and so once in a while they would come down and raid the Pimas."[7] Later in the book he reflects on these traditional enemies: Some people say the Apaches were bad, Webb says, but he is not so sure. They raided the Pimas for food, but, he adds,

> They never tried to drive us off our land and away from our homes. We never tried to drive them out of their own country.
> But the white man did.
> If you were an Apache what do you think you would have done?[8]

Webb goes on to add that history has shown that virtually every group, Indians as well as whites, has tried to take things from other groups. The point he makes earlier still stands, however: The "white man" took acquisitiveness to a level not seen among Indian tribes, and Apache resistance must be seen in that context.

When Webb discusses the Pimas people's first contact with white settlers, he once again focuses on Pima generosity as he describes early trading encounters. The whites offered cloth and beads for the food the Pimas grew, but this was not exactly a case of naive Indians being lured by white trade goods: "The beads pleased the Pimas, but to help these strangers pleased them more. That is how the Pimas are. They have never been good traders."[9] The rest of Webb's description of Pima-white relations maintains the same spirit. Settlers and soldiers underestimate the talents, energy, and wisdom of the Pimas, but eventually come to realize that "the Pimas' natural civilization was not so different from what they were trying to teach their own children."[10]

For Webb, Christianity was readily accepted by the Pimas because it represents another version of the morality inherent in Pima culture. The generosity, hospitality, honesty, and humility of the Pimas fit well with Christianity as they perceived it. He includes stories about the Pimas' ability to laugh at themselves as a central part of his discussion of religion, and he ends that discussion with a statement that epitomizes his own approach to religion: "One thing I am sure of. The smarter a man is the more he needs God to protect him from thinking he knows everything."[11] Within the context of the narrative, it seems clear that this is also a message for the representatives of white civilization.

Webb saves his direct criticism of European American behavior for the last part of the book. After telling short but engaging versions of several Pima legends, he entitles his next chapter, "The Legend of Today." This legend, which the Pimas are living out, is "harder to believe" than the old stories. He points out that most of the changes in the Pima way of life were, to his mind, superficial:

> The people put on clothes and hats, built adobe houses, learned English, and bought groceries in a grocery store. They had wagons and horses and became Christians, and went hunting with rifles instead of bows and arrows. All these things were unimportant because they still farmed and brought in good harvests.[12]

I think this passage is central to understanding Webb's book and Pima culture in general. The Pimas are defined, not by religion in a conventional sense or even by the outward signs of culture, though those factors certainly play an important role. They are farmers, and most of what they value springs from that: The generosity, the hospitality, the humility, the order and structure of Pima life are rooted in the ability to farm the land successfully and to share what they grow. As long as their identity as growers of good crops was intact, the core of their culture was safe from outside influences. Unfortunately, the ability to farm is definitely one of the things that white culture is stealing from them as Webb writes *A Pima Remembers*.

As he reflects on the differences between traditional and modern life, he clearly shows that the Pima have not really gained from their contact with white settlers. In one of the few overtly sarcastic passages in the book, he points out that, like whites, Pimas can now get drunk and kill themselves on the highway; like whites, they can fret about making payments on television sets and can play around and ruin their marriages. "Yes," he concludes, "The Pima Indian is getting civilized."[13] Still, Webb adds, the real reason he would prefer living in the traditional way is what has happened to land and water.

The story of land is soon told. White speculators try to buy Pima land in spite of government protections; the state wants it taken out of reservation hands so it can be taxed; some Pimas themselves want to sell because they are unable to make a living as farmers and need money. Unlike Anna Moore Shaw, who is enthusiastic about the prospects for "development" on the Pima reservation, Webb is extremely distrustful of those who would buy and/or develop Pima land, and he feels that the reservation system protects Pima traditions by prohibiting land sales.

The real story, though, is water, and this is dealt with in Webb's concluding chapter. As long as the Pima people had water, Webb says, they could adapt to changing circumstances and maintain community. Water was distributed to those who needed it most, and everyone worked together to repair dams and ditches. The whole valley of the Gila River was green with Pima crops, Webb says, and he adds, "All this was the result of helping each other, and having plenty of water from the Gila River."[14] Clearly, water and community go together, and the complex network of ditches and dams, built and maintained by the Pimas over centuries, represents the vascular system that has nourished Pima life and culture. As long as that system of water distribution was intact, the Pimas would survive as a people in a changing world.

The building of the first dam upstream from the Pima reservation robbed the people of that system. Crops failed, livestock died, farmland turned to desert, groves of cottonwoods died and fell. When the Pimas dug wells they soon dried up from the lowering of the water table. Trying to remain on the land, many Pimas sold wood from the mesquite trees that quickly became rare on the reservation. Coolidge Dam, which was theoretically intended to provide water to the reservation, helped for about five years after it was completed: Then white speculators who had bought land below the dam managed to get most of the river water and drilled wells that further lowered the water table. Meanwhile the Pimas were accused by whites of being lazy because they could not farm their land or of stealing water from whites when they dug wells of their own. Webb's portrait of the reservation after these changes is affectingly poetic. He remembers the time when the ditches flowed and water ran to the melons, alfalfa, and corn. The red-winged blackbirds, whose song always means that there is water nearby, "would sing in the trees and fly down to look for bugs along the ditches."

> Now the river is an empty bed full of sand.
> Now you can stand in that same place and see the wind tearing pieces of bark off

the cottonwood trees along the dry ditches.

The trees stand there like white bones. The red-winged blackbirds have gone somewhere else. Mesquite and brush and tumbleweeds have begun to turn those Pima fields into desert.[15]

In Webb's view, it is not the government that is to blame, except insofar as it turns a blind eye to individual injustice now and then. The real problem is the greed of ordinary whites, which Webb describes in a typically disarming way:

I had two years in business school, but only last year I let a white man take me on a business deal for two thousand dollars.
And he had never been to high school.[16]

The implication is clear. The problem springs, not from education, but from cultural values—the Pimas with their generosity and humility have never been "good traders." Whites who are willing to practice greed and dishonesty have an edge in that area. However, becoming "Americans" is not a viable option for the Pimas. Webb ends his book by suggesting that "the pace of what is called progress" is too much even for whites. It baffles "a simple Pima who remembers the Gila river when it was a running stream."[17] Clearly, Webb is not nearly as simple as he might seem to be, and the ending of the book shows a powerful ability to use language to bring home the injustice and sadness of the situation. The running stream of the Gila becomes the image that defines Webb's identity as a Pima, and it is clear that, in taking that water, white culture has also shaken the foundation of Pima culture.

The incursion of white culture and the loss of viable farmland and farming traditions have had an even more direct life-threatening effect as well. When Anna Moore Shaw describes the appearance of the first Christian missionary on the reservation, she unwittingly provides a disturbing symbol for that effect. Charles H. Cook, a Christian hero in Shaw's book, studied Pima culture and language and then "began to teach the children by giving them crackers and cube sugar."[18] However benevolent Cook's intentions may have been in Shaw's view, his enticements symbolize one of the deadliest developments in the relationship between the Pima people and mainstream American culture. When a team from the National Institutes of Health came to the Gila River Valley Reservation in the early 1960s, they planned to study rheumatoid arthritis, but their focus quickly shifted when they discovered that more than half of the Pimas over the age of thirty, and 80 percent of those older than fifty-five, had type 2 diabetes. The influence of white culture and the loss of the water from the Gila and Salt Rivers had changed the diets and activity levels of the people. In place of traditional, high-fiber and low-fat foods such as tepary beans, corn, and squash supplemented with low-fat meat from game and grass-fed cattle, the Pima diet shifted to include high levels of fats, sugars, and refined flour. In addition, the active lifestyle required by farming gave way to a sedentary one in many cases. The so-called "thrifty genes," which enable Pimas and other American Indian peoples to store fat in times of food shortage, became a deadly heritage in this new context, as 80 percent of the population became overweight, the highest single risk factor in type 2 diabetes.[19]

The Pima response was typically generous. Called upon to help researchers study the disease, the Pima people have responded in ways that reflect their emphasis on cooperation and helpfulness. Ninety percent of the Pima people have participated in a study of type 2 diabetes that has lasted for nearly 40 years. Those who study the issue of type 2 diabetes often express their amazement at this level of participation. The words of Francine Kaufman—past president of the American Diabetes Association and a professor of pediatrics at the University of Southern California who has done extensive work in the field of what has come to be called "Diabesity"—reflect the view of many researchers regarding the Pima people's cooperation in the study of the disease:

> They've been interviewed and examined; they've been weighed and measured for height. They've kept activity diaries, worn heart rate monitors, swallowed glucose solutions, and provided blood samples. Some have spent days isolated in special chambers so their metabolism could be measured precisely.[20]

In fact, most of our understanding of type 2 diabetes—its genetic component, its relationship to diet and exercise, its effects on organs and internal systems—come from this kind of cooperation among the Pima people. As Kaufman says, "We all owe much to the Pimas' generosity."[21]

This generosity has become even more important as the entire U.S. population faces an epidemic of "diabesity." Before the mid-1990s, type 2 diabetes was so rare in children that it was generally called "adult-onset" diabetes. By 1997 this form of diabetes had become so common among children that the American Diabetes Association recommended that the term "adult onset diabetes" be replaced.[22] As I suggested above in the introduction to this book, the damage we do to American Indian cultures rebounds on us like the witchery that Leslie Marmon Silko describes in *Ceremony*. The crackers and sugar that missionaries (both religious and cultural) brought to the Pimas, along with the destruction of farming traditions, has led to our own cultural crisis as well. The widespread disappearance of farming as a way of life, and the changes in our diet, consumption patterns, and exercise habits, all brought about in the name of progress, profit, and efficiency, have undermined our own health and that of future generations. In our damming of the Gila and our undermining of Pima prosperity and health, we have laid the seeds of our own suffering and possible demise, and the dry sand of the Gila symbolizes the sometimes disastrous interconnectedness of our worlds.

The Water Returns

Fortunately, the story does not end there. On an August evening in 2006, my fiancée and I are sitting across the table from Robert Stone, the first Akimel O'Odham manager of the Gila River Farms since 1968, when the job was given to white farm managers. He wears his black hair in a long braid down his back but is dressed in a T-shirt, hiking shorts, and tennis shoes. His whole face, with its wispy mustache and prominent eyes, is lit by a glowing smile. "It's running," he says. "The Gila is running right now." The drought that has withered Arizona and the rest of the Southwest for the last seven years has been interrupted by heavy "monsoon" rains, and the dry wash that the Gila has been for decades is running strongly with brown flood water. Once the rains end in a month or so, the water will dry up for now, but the symbolism is appropriate, because I have asked Robert (or "Bobby" as he more often calls himself) to talk to me about plans for the water that will soon be returning to the Pima farmlands.

This return of the water is a testament to quiet Pima persistence. Since 1925 the Pimas have presented their claims to Gila River water in federal court, spending millions of dollars in an attempt to get their water back. The effort has finally paid off: In December 2004, President Bush signed into law the Arizona Water Settlements Act, which gives the Pima people an allocation of 650,000 acre-feet of water, more than three times the amount they have been using. The settlement represents some compromises, of course: The water will come, not from restoring the flow of the Gila, but from Central Arizona Project (CAP) canals, which bring water from the Colorado River; the Pima people will receive less water than they asked for, but the federal government will pay for the construction of a distribution system (an important point, since several tribes have in the past received rights to water that they cannot use without huge and unaffordable construction projects.) The act has also been criticized by some tribal advocates because it limits the amount of water the Pimas can lease to their non-Indian neighbors and sets a formula for the price they can charge. In general, though, most of the Pima people see the act as an opportunity to restore some of the farming tradition that was lost in the years of little water.

If Bobby Stone has his way, that is exactly what it will do. We first met when I brought a group of students to the Southwest for a travel seminar in the summer of 2004, about six months before the passage of the Water Settlements Act. He is the kind of person who can competently manage a huge modern farming operation and yet find time to learn the special language of traditional songs, which is different from spoken Pima, so he can be a singer for basket dances. He impressed us with his creative ideas for the farm—encouraging community gardens, cultivating more traditional foods, developing organic crops. When we left his office he sent us off with a gift, a case of plump grapefruit from the Gila Farms orchards, and that evening he joined us for dinner at the Gila River Cultural Center and sang for the dancers.

In 2006 the students spent more time with Bobby. He was bubbling over with ideas for the water that had officially been won in 2004. A local dairy wants organic feed, and that will provide the impetus to use some of the fields that have been out of production to grow organic sorghum and eventually other organic crops. He wants a garden at the cultural center to show the importance of agriculture to Pima history and culture. A Hohokam village which was recently discovered, carefully documented, and then reburied because it included human remains could be recreated along the Gila, and that section of the river could have flowing water: The government has programs that encourage sending water down dry riverbeds in order to recharge the dwindling underground aquifers. Such a recreation would enable Pima students and others to understand the role of water in history, Stone says, and children could experience the role of water in a thriving community rather than just read about it.

Indeed, the importance of teaching Pima children about their own heritage is central to his plans: He wants to encourage and expand programs such as the award winning garden project at Gila Crossing Community School, where children grow traditional crops on the school grounds and in the process learn about the dangers of diabetes as well as learning from tribal elders the Pima names for the seeds and the traditional ways of growing them. The produce grown at the school is served at the Sheraton Hotel located in the tribe's resort complex at Wild Horse Pass. He is particularly concerned with getting children involved with agriculture and tied to the land. In addition to providing summer jobs in agriculture, water from the farm has been used to keep alive groves of the cottonwood trees whose dying forms haunt George Webb's prose. In Bobby Stone's view the trees represent a living link to the past for younger generations: "That's history; that's got to keep going," he says. The section of the Gila River that is used for recharge would provide outdoor recreation, and a thriving and expanding farm would let students know that they could use the skills they learn in school without having to leave the reservation, working with computers, using engineering skills in construction projects, doing marketing for farm products, using GPS knowledge in future planning. Future students will know that they will not have to choose between possible unemployment on the reservation and the trauma of finding a way of surviving in the foreign and often hostile world of Phoenix or Tucson.

When I ask him what he would most like to see when the water returns, he echoes George Webb: "The whole valley green, like it used to be," he says without hesitation. There will have to be the big commercial farm, he adds, but he would like to see lots of smaller, more traditional farms as well. He would also like to see the mesquite trees come back and the desert animals return.

One of his most interesting ideas is a monument to the Japanese who were interned on the reservation during World War II. The Pima people already have a display focusing on the internment camp in their cultural center, and during our tour of the farm, Bobby took us to the site of the camp and talked about how much sympathy the Pimas had for the Japanese and how much they appreciated the gardens the Japanese established during their stay in Arizona. Some Pima elders do not want to call attention to problems from the past, he says, but he wants the Japanese story to be told. That, I think, represents typical Pima generosity.

As our dinner arrives, Bobby Stone tells us that he would like to pay for it. I start to protest, but then I catch myself. Generosity clearly makes him happy, and rather than struggle against it, I make a mental note to emulate it and send him some Arkansas honey when we get back home. As we finish our interview, he gets on the subject of the wild horses on the reservation, which must occasionally be rounded up to keep their numbers in check. He understands the need for controlling the numbers, he says, but he wants the horses to remain as part of the reservation population. "I tell people that there's a mystic warrior on each one of those horses," he says. "And they're saying, 'We're going to be here; we're going to stay here.'"

Pima Culture in the Classroom

By studying the Pimas, then, students can learn a number of important things. First, looking at the Pima creation story in the context of cultural history can show students that creation stories can be richly meaningful when we approach them, not as descriptions of "what happened," but as descriptions of cultural values. This is not to reduce the stories to illustrations of moral truths or to denigrate their role within the culture as descriptions of history. In my experience, American Indians, like Christians, have varying individual perspectives on the literal truth of creation stories. For example, when I said something to my travel seminar about the scientific view that corn had been carefully domesticated from an unknown species of grass, our Hopi guide, a woman who has a master's degree in museum studies, responded, "We believe that blue corn was given to us by Massau." That was an important reminder to me that for many American Indian people—even to those who have studied the European American academic approach to cultures and history—creation stories are historical. On the other hand, it is also important to remember that the "Big Bang" is itself a creation story, no matter how many highly educated people believe it to be the one and only literal truth. We must remember that stories work in mysterious ways, and students can miss important meanings if they focus only on the literal level of creation stories that are different from their own. Both the conservative Christian students and the scientific fundamentalists, who make up the greater part of my classes, are often inclined to dismiss non-Christian or "unscientific" stories as "false" because they do not correspond to the literal description they have been given. Both groups can benefit from an approach that focuses on the ways in which all creation stories tell about who the people are as well as how they came to be who they are. The Pima stories, with their emphasis on humility and the avoidance of conflict, can help students to see that more clearly when they are read in a cultural context, and they can serve as a basis for examining our assumptions about what is "true."

Reading *A Pima Remembers* can further promote cultural understanding, and it can also get students to see in a fairly unthreatening way just how European American culture has damaged and destroyed traditional values, not necessarily out of some malicious genocidal urge (however much that urge may have played a role in some other contexts), but because of the value we place on being "good traders" and the effect that value had on a culture that defines itself as "good neighbors." The best evidence for our lack of cultural awareness, as I have suggested earlier, is the ways in which we have treated ourselves almost as badly as we have treated the Pimas, driving our own families off farms and creating an epidemic of diabetes among our own children. Within this context, it is also vitally important for students to know about the generosity of the Pima people as manifested in their participation in studies that are enabling us to understand this disease of diabesity that comes with our way of life.

Finally, the victory of the Pimas in their battle for water can help to undermine the perception of American Indians as victims or as members of cultures that must either vanish (except insofar as we preserve them as artifacts in museums and texts), or assimilate because their way of life is outmoded. It is certainly true that the Pimas have been cheated and mistreated. Their desire to help their European American neighbors was clearly betrayed by the settlers who took advantage of their peacefulness and generosity. Looking back, George Webb could understand the Apaches' choice to resist American settlers with violence. The Pimas have had to change and adapt in many ways just to survive. Nevertheless, the Pima people are still here, they are still Pimas, and they are getting their water back. In the words of Bobby Stone, they are telling us, "We're going to be here; we're going to stay here."

Chapter 6

American Indian Literature as World Literature: "Yellow Woman" and *Smoke Signals*

Defining "World Literature"

I begin this chapter with a confession that will also introduce the problem to be addressed: I received a Ph.D. in American Literature without ever having read a single work written by an American Indian. This was not entirely the fault of the universities I attended. Both the University of Arizona and the University of California, Los Angeles, had among their faculty pioneers in the field of American Indian Literature—Larry Evers and Kenneth Lincoln, respectively. For me as a graduate student, however, American Indian literature was "a field," a speciality that was outside my "areas of interest." Moreover, it was not included in undergraduate (or graduate) courses in American literature. When I discovered American Indian literature as a teacher, I realized just how exclusive our approach to categorizing literature can be, and I am determined that none of my students will ever be able to make the same confession. American Indian literature is part of every American Literature course I teach.

Indeed, the general education requirements at my university give me a chance to go even further. Every student at the University of Central Arkansas has to take a course in World Literature, and many take both halves of the two-semester sequence—the ancient world through the sixteenth century and the seventeenth century (more or less) to the modern period. Although our emphasis on world literature is part of a long-standing commitment to a traditional General Education curriculum, it also fits very well with the new focus on expanding curricula to include more literature from non-European cultures, both at the university level and in the public schools: An emphasis on globalization has led many universities to expand their offerings in the literatures of other countries and cultures, and junior and senior high school teachers in Arkansas are finding more and more "non-western" works in their literature anthologies. Because those same anthologies are used nationally, I think we can conclude that students who go on to teach in public schools will encounter world literatures in their curricula. As I regularly teach the second half of the two-semester sequence—World Literature II, as it is called—I decided that American Indian literature should have a place in my version of the course. The Norton Anthology that we use includes a small selection of oral materials—a bit of the Navajo Night Chant, three Zuni ritual prayers, some Inuit songs—and "Yellow Woman," by Leslie Marmon Silko. I am happy for these inclusions: When I began teaching American literature in 1982, there was no significant evidence in any Norton anthology that American Indian cultures ever existed, and "world" literature meant the literature of France, Italy, and Germany, as well as that of England and the United States. Context is important to me, however, and this small and miscellaneous selection does not give a very clear sense of the richness and complexity of American Indian cultures and literatures or of the way in which those cultures are struggling for survival in modern America.

 A related issue that arises in teaching "world" literature is coherence. How does a teacher represent a body of work so huge and various as the literature of the world in a way that gives students some sense of relationship and connection? The course can quickly degenerate into a series of unrelated literary works, each of which represents a different culture, without any sense of continuity or contrast that will enable students to see relationships. Clearly, the instructor needs some way to set up a basis for comparison and continuity.

The Journey

I decided on the journey story as a way of approaching both of these challenges. The journey is one metaphor for the human encounter with the world in every culture I have studied, and, I thought, by looking at the way in which the journey is depicted in different cultures, one might be able to suggest grounds for comparison: a way of looking at, and understanding the significance of, differences and similarities within a common structure. In addition, because the journey can be either literal or metaphorical, the idea of journey enables us to look at a wide range of works. The Chinese story, *Monkey,* and Voltaire's *Candide*, with their literal journeys, can be studied along with Blake's metaphorical depiction of the journey from innocence through experience to organized innocence and Frederick Douglass's double journey from South to North and from slavery to freedom in his *Narrative of the Life of an American Slave*. The Norton Anthology also offers an Indian work, Premchand's "Road to Salvation" and an Egyptian one, Naguib Mahfouz's "Zaabalawi," as examples of spiritual journeys from Hindu and Sufi perspectives, respectively. Silko's "Yellow Woman" is perhaps the most interesting example of all, because it takes the traditional journey of Yellow Woman as it appears in ancient Pueblo stories and recasts it in a modern setting.

The journey motif enables the course to focus on the nature of story as well, for it is not the journey itself but telling the story of the journey that helps to define the cultural perspective. The historical journey of a Chinese priest who travels to India in order to bring Buddhist scriptures to China, for example, becomes the allegorical *Journey to the West* and then the shorter *Monkey*, as the story is retold through many generations and finally translated into English by Arthur Whaley. The journey that Douglass made from slavery to freedom was not unique, but his ability to shape that journey into a compelling story for a northern audience made his narrative into an important and powerful experience for his readers, an experience which contributed to the abolition of slavery and still offers insight into American history and the African American perspective. Indeed, Douglass was so determined to tell his story that he published his narrative knowing that he would have to flee the country when it appeared, thus showing how strongly he believed that effectively telling his story would help abolish slavery.

Stories, moreover, are an important aspect of the journey itself, since often the crucial points on the journey are embodied in stories. In some ways *Monkey*, for example, is a journey from story to story as well as from place to place. To give a single instance, the story of the king of Crow Cock featured in the Norton Anthology begins with the king telling his story to Tripitaka, the monk who is leading the expedition to China. Then we learn through the course of three chapters that the king's is only one version of the whole story of Crow Cock. The episode is, among other things, a story about stories—about the way we can be misled when we have only one version of a story. William Blake's depiction of innocence and experience consists in stories told by chimney sweepers, a little black boy, a child tutoring a lamb, and other characters passing from innocence to experience. Once again, it is up to us to bring our own experience to the stories, to understand how society will turn each innocent speaker into an experienced and disillusioned one, and how the expereinced speaker also has only a partial view of the world. Each person encountered by the narrator in Mahfouz's "Zaabalawi" has a story to tell about the elusive title character, and the stories define each character's relationship to the healing vision represented by the mysterious Zaabalawi. The stories we tell and hear are the milestones on our journeys and show the way we have come.

With these ideas in mind, *Smoke Signals*, a film written and directed by American Indian artists Sherman Alexie and Chris Eyre, struck me as a logical addition to the course. It tells the story of a journey, which is also very consciously a journey made of stories, as Thomas Builds-the-Fire redefines Victor Joseph's father for him and thus helps Victor complete the journey toward maturity. Moreover, as a retelling of "This Is What It Means to Say Phoenix, Arizona," it shows Sherman Alexie's revisiting of his own story and documents his journey as a writer from the time of *The Lone Ranger and Tonto Fistfight in Heaven* to the making of the film. In Blake's terms it represents Alexie's own journey from the experienced and sometimes bitter perspective in the earlier work to a fuller view of his own struggles. In this chapter, then, I would like to make the case for including American Indian works such as "Yellow Woman" and *Smoke Signals* as world literature, and I will also venture to suggest one way in which that might be done by focusing on journeys.

Creating a Context

In my experience, students need extra help in order to deal with American Indian works, even if they have spent most of a semester reading works from various cultures. I think that the first hurdle in teaching Silko's story, for example, is the difference in perspectives on what we call the natural world. The very term, *nature*, implies that we are one kind of thing and everything around us is another kind of thing: Here am I, and there is nature. Silko addresses this issue in her essay, "Interior and Exterior Landscapes," when she points out that the very concept of landscape is foreign to the Pueblo way of thinking: "Viewers are as much a part of the landscape as the boulders they stand on. There is no high mesa edge or mountain peak where one can stand and not immediately be part of all that surrounds."[1] As Patricia Clark Smith and Paula Gunn Allen put it, "For [American Indian peoples] the land is not just a collection of objects you do things *to*, nor is it merely a place you do things *in*, a stage set for human action. Rather, it is a multitude of entities who possess intelligence and personality."[2] From the Pueblo perspective, we are not people acting within a world of things; we are one kind of people interacting with other kinds of people, and a place is the sum of these interactions.

We see a similar perspective in "Yellow Woman" as the narrator leaves her domestic world of school buses, police cars, and Jello to follow a mysterious stranger named Silva who insists that he is a mountain Kaatsina like the one who kidnapped Yellow Woman in the Kochininako stories. She tries to explain why she goes with the mysterious stranger in words that show Silko's view: "I did not decide to go. I just went. Moonflowers blossom in the sand hills before dawn, just as I followed him."[3] The human action of the story, then, neither occurs "in nature" nor is influenced "by nature." Rather, it is as much a part of what we would call nature as the blossoming of flowers.

In order to introduce students to this perspective we read the Zuni "Prayer at the Winter Solstice" and a Cherokee journey story called "The Bear Man." We discuss the way in which traditional American Indian people live in a world of other persons, not a world of objects. When the Zuni pray to their mothers— the earth and the corn—they are not using metaphorical language, exactly, except insofar as all language is metaphorical. The earth and the corn are felt to be conscious and living relatives without whose love and gifts the people would not be able to live. I tell students about Sunny Dooley, a Navajo storyteller we have listened to several times as part of a Southwest travel course, who tells us that before she built her hogan she had to make offerings of cornmeal from a special basket and ask permission from the animals (including the ants) who lived in the space she wanted to use. Her father also vetoed her first choice for a site because the "water beings" had claimed it. Clearly, traditional Navajo and Pueblo peoples see themselves as human persons living side by side with other persons (stones, clouds, trees, ants), all of whom constitute a place.

Within this world, stories define the relationships among the persons who comprise the place. When the protagonist in the Cherokee story of the Bear Man is invited to live with the bear, for example, he is experiencing the story that defines the relationship between bear people and Cherokee people. The bear gives his "clothes" (his fur and flesh) to the Cherokee, and in return he expects understanding and the observance of ceremonial behavior (covering his blood with leaves), which embodies the people's respect. When that respect is given, the bear will return with his gifts.[4] Silko makes a similar point in her essay when she writes of the antelope: "The antelope merely consents to return home with the hunter. All phases of the hunt are conducted with love."[5] If that love is violated through carelessness, the animals will not return. Though the Bear Man dies at the end of the story because he is not given seven days alone to let the bear nature leave him—a further indication of both the closeness and the distinctions between different "peoples"—the story of his journey survives after the hunter's death and continues to describe the way in which the Cherokee people must interact with the bear people.

In this context, the critical discussion about the ambiguous nature of the narrator's experience in "Yellow Woman" can perhaps be misleading. While it is true that the narrator shows some confusion about her relationship to the traditional story of Yellow Woman, that confusion, I think, is a product of a modern world in which stories are denigrated and often denied their significance. From Silko's Laguna perspective, stories are what happens in the world. When Silko's narrator objects that the Yellow Woman stories happened long ago, Silva tells her, "But someday they will talk about us, and they will say, 'Those two lived long ago when things like that happened.'"[6] We relive the stories even when, like their original characters, we are unaware that what we are doing is a story. As old Grandma says at the end of *Ceremony*, "It seems like I already heard these stories before . . . only thing is, the names sound different."[7]

Moreover, Silko affirms the universal nature of the stories explicitly in interviews, and implicitly in *Gardens in the Dunes*, when she has her characters read *Monkey* on their own journey from California to New York and then to Europe, and when she draws parallels among American Indian stories, Celtic and Italian myth, Christianity and the Ghost Dance, and the lives of her twentieth-century characters. Silko's perspective invites us to explore the Yellow Woman story as one particular manifestation of the journey that appears in every culture. Like the Egyptian narrator in Mahfouz's "Zaabalawi," who seeks healing from "that illness for which no one possesses a remedy,"[8] and like the feuding Hindu characters in Premchand's story who find "The Road to Salvation," when they have lost both the material goods they valued and the pride that sprang from those possessions and find that "there was nothing left to be angry about,"[9] Silko's narrator is taken from the world of everyday experience in order to connect with a deeper reality.

"Yellow Woman"—An American Indian Perspective

At the same time, the differences among the stories are also highly instructive: Mahfouz's Muslim narrator and Premchand's Hindu characters journey within human society. The unnamed narrator in "Zaabalawi" seeks healing in the social world of Cairo, asking advice from a lawyer, a bookseller, a municipal official, an artist, and a composer, and finally getting a glimpse of what he seeks from a drunkard who insists that the narrator drink wine until he loses control—a Sufi metaphor for the loss of self that leads to the discovery that God is within. In "The Road to Salvation," a farmer and a shepherd try to destroy each other until neither has anything left to lose and both find peace, thus demonstrating both a version of the Hindu path to enlightenment and Premchand's concern with a social situation in which members of the peasant castes fight each other instead of focusing on their common suffering. Neither story shows the deep connection to the mountains and rivers, the pines and gray squirrels that informs "Yellow Woman." As Patricia Clark Smith argues, the Yellow Woman stories portray "an inevitable human need to go forth and experience wilderness—and the sexual wildness that it encompasses."[10] It is this reconnection with wildness that the story brings to the culture, both in its traditional forms and in Silko's retelling. Looking at the three stories together, then, can demonstrate the ways in which American Indian stories are connected to the human story of the journey and at the same time illustrate the characteristics that make each culture unique in its way of embodying the journey.

To focus more specifically on "Yellow Woman," one major difficulty my students have is the apparent adultery with which the story begins. Our narrator tells us in a matter-of-fact way that she is lying on the sand thigh-to-thigh with a man who, we soon learn, is not her husband. Moreover, she has a child at home. Students sometimes become so focused on this violation of their moral standards that it must be dealt with before we can move on. I turn the situation into a chance to do some cultural detective work. If the author is apparently not inviting us to condemn our narrator for this behavior—something that students can see fairly easily—then how might Pueblo views of marriage and gender roles differ from ours? In her essay, "Yellow Woman and a Beauty of the Spirit," Silko addresses these cultural differences, pointing out that gender roles and sexual mores were much more flexible in Pueblo society before Christianity came than they are in American society. Sexuality and fertility were valued highly, and individual differences were respected. Marriage was about "teamwork and social relationships" rather than sexual possession, and women were as likely as men to take lovers. Because a child belonged to its mother's clan, there was no problem of illegitimacy—every child was cared for. In the traditional stories, in fact, Yellow Woman sometimes falls in love with an abductor and even returns from an adventure with Whirlwind Man carrying twin children, who become Pueblo heroes. For Silko, the story of Yellow Woman celebrates sensuality and shows how it can benefit the people: "her power lies in her courage and in her uninhibited sexuality, which the old-time Pueblo stories celebrate again and again because fertility was so highly valued."[11]

In an interview given in 1986, Silko adds another level to the meaning of Yellow Woman's sensuality. When Kim Barnes asks her if her story is about a kind of feminist rebellion against a male-dominated world, Silko disagrees emphatically. That reading of the story arises from circumstances in white middle-class society. In Pueblo culture, women have tremendous social importance and take on jobs that American culture sees as masculine. There is no male domination to rebel against. Rather, Silko says, Yellow Woman shows "this attraction, this passion, this connection between the human world and the animal and spirit worlds."[12] Her sexual attraction to the ka'tsina is a metaphor for the human and non-human worlds being drawn together.

When the narrator goes with Silva—the name means literally a miscellany or a kind of poem but also suggests "sylvan"—she experiences the world the way it was before buses and Jello and policemen. From Silva's cabin in the mountains she sees no sign of the changes that have been made by the coming of white culture. She also encounters in Silva a defiant spirit that refuses to accept domination by American culture. Silko insists in many places that American culture owes a debt to the American Indian cultures whose lands have been stolen. By hunting the cattle that replaced the game that sustained the people, Silva is collecting on that debt. His defeat of the white rancher who tries to arrest him is implied in the four shots the narrator hears as she flees the confrontation between the men. Four is the sacred number of completion in Pueblo culture (and many other American Indian traditions). It seems unlikely that we are to assume that Silva has killed the rancher—the white man is unarmed, and one would expect Silva to be a one-shot hunter. Rather, I think, we are to hear in the four shots the ceremonial triumph of the wild spirit of the mountains over the culture that thinks it can dominate that spirit. As Silko says in several places, American Indian prophecies predict the eventual disappearance, not of Europeans, but of European customs and perspectives from the Americas. The land will eventually assert its primacy, despite the efforts of European culture to desecrate it. "Humans desecrate only themselves," she adds. "The earth is inviolate."[13]

If, as Silko suggests, Yellow Woman acts in a time of crisis in order to bring important gifts to her people,[14] how might we understand Silko's retelling of the story? What is the crisis facing the people, and what is it that her modern-day Yellow Woman brings when she returns? I think the crisis is inherent in the narrator's view of stories. The adventures of Yellow Woman, she insists at first, happened long ago. In a world of Jello and school buses she has been led to accept a linear view of time. In a 1995 interview with Tomas Irmer and Matthias Schmidt, Silko describes the quite different Pueblo view of time: "The Pueblo people and the indigenous people of the Americas see time as round," she says. Given this view of time as more like an ocean than a string of events, "something that happened five hundred years ago may be quite immediate and real."[15] The narrator, on the other hand, sees pickup trucks and policemen as real because they are part of her immediate surroundings, whereas Yellow Woman's adventures are not part of reality because they happened so long ago. In the course of her adventure, however, the narrator comes to understand that the Yellow Woman story is part of present reality. She expresses her disappointment that her grandfather will not be there to hear her adventure, because "it was the Yellow Woman stories he liked to tell best."[16] As a traditional Pueblo man, her grandfather would have realized that his granddaughter's adventure was the story of Yellow Woman, which is always near at hand in the ocean of time. Because she is willing to act on the sensual attraction of the mountain spirit, which metaphorically represents the connection to the animal and spirit worlds, the narrator renews the presence of the story and brings it back to the people.

Smoke Signals—*Stereotypes and Stories*

Adding *Smoke Signals* to the mix further enriches the students' experience of the cultural complexities related to stories. It is important to look closely at different contemporary American Indian writers in order to underscore the differences between peoples who are lumped together in the European American imagination. Our stories about the "Indians," the film insists, are much too simple. Indeed, in many ways, *Smoke Signals* is a work specifically designed to explode stereotypes and show the deeper truth underlying them. The Coeur d'Alene characters in the film show their vivid awareness of the popular image of the Indian: "We're Indians, remember? We barter," says the young woman who offers a ride to Victor and Thomas. Victor's lesson for Thomas on how to look like an Indian is a hilarious collection of stereotypical images. "You have to look like you've just got back from killing a buffalo," Victor says. When Thomas points out that Coeur d'Alene people are fishermen, Victor responds, "You want to look like you just came back from catching a fish? It isn't *Dances with Salmon*, you know."

Victor believes that, as American Indians interacting with mainstream America, he and Thomas have to protect themselves by acting out the stereotype of the fierce Indian brave, a stereotype that allows no room for differences between American Indian cultures, let alone individual temperaments. This view is given the lie in one of the most engaging moments of the film: As Victor and the bus driver wait, Thomas emerges from a store near where the bus has stopped, his long unbraided hair flowing, his "stoic" face radiating the tough and enduring expressionlessness that Victor has demanded he assume. He looks like the Indian that Victor (and American culture) wants him to be. Then he puts his glasses on and a radiant smile lights his face, and we are reminded that, however much he may be an "Indian," he is Thomas.

Victor's bitterness about American culture and his determination to show only toughness and a hard exterior are founded in his experience of "being an Indian in the twentieth century," an offense that Thomas says is punishable by imprisonment. That experience includes the natural beauty of the reservation, an aspect that Alexie considers an important part of the film's perspective, but it also includes alcoholism, abuse, poverty, and alienation—all aspects of the beauty and the pain behind the stereotype. His father's suffering and ultimate disappearance have left Victor unable to trust anyone and contemptuous of Thomas's stories about Arnold Joseph. Victor's most frequent line in the movie is, "Thomas, you're so full of shit." Thus, the journey to Phoenix is a mythic trek, a journey to reclaim a father and a heritage rooted in stories. The story begins with the fire that kills Thomas's parents, a fire which is accidentally started by Arnold Joseph and which leaves him carrying the unbearable guilt for those deaths; it ends when Victor completes the connection to his own metaphorical Phoenix and can rise from the ashes of his bitterness and deal with the literal ashes of his father.

The film does a wonderful job of using the imagery of fire and ash to frame the meaning of the journey. From Thomas's voiceover at the beginning to the final scene of Victor scattering his father's ashes into the Spokane River, the film stays with its central metaphor to create a depth that is rare in American movies. The house fire unites Victor and Thomas, because Arnold Joseph is both the accidental killer of Thomas's parents and the similarly inadvertent savior of Thomas's life. Thomas accepts the connection in his socially inept way, telling Victor, and anyone else who will listen, endless stories about Arnold. Victor, on the other hand, burns with anger against Thomas, who seems to have a deeper connection to Arnold than he has. As Victor yells just before the climactic car crash on the way back from Phoenix, "He saved your ass from that fire. He didn't save me."

At the same time, Victor is reluctant to accept that father, and he reaffirms Thomas's claim on Arnold by silently urging Thomas to take the canister of ashes held out to Victor by Suzy Song, the woman who befriends Arnold in Phoenix and passes on his earthly remains. As with the stories that Thomas offers, the ashes represent a challenge to claim his problematic relationship to his father (and his heritage), a challenge that Victor cannot accept through most of the movie. Even after he enters his father's trailer and cuts his hair as a sign of mourning, Victor is still filled with bitterness. As Thomas suggests, he has not really finished the ceremony of healing. It takes the car accident and Victor's marathon run to get help to complete what has only been started in the journey to Phoenix. Having sacrificed himself in order to save a woman's life, Victor can truly connect with his father and answer the local lawman's question about the contents of the canister in a way that asserts that connection: "That's my father," he says. Then, as he and Thomas get ready to drive back home in Arnold's pickup, Victor asks Thomas for the canister: "Let me hold Dad for a while," he says. Victor has finally completed the ceremony and is ready for the journey home. When the two boys get into the pickup, Victor mirrors his father's action in a previous scene, anxiously encouraging the engine to fire as the starter cranks futilely. In a brilliant use of montage, this scene is intercut with images of Suzy Song trying to light a bundle of sage so she can set fire to Arnold's trailer. The sage and the pickup engine finally both fire up at the same time, linking the ceremonial burning of Arnold's earthly effects with Victor's acceptance of what his father has bequeathed him, and showing his readiness to return to the reservation in Arnold's yellow pickup. Paradoxically, the scene uses the metaphor of ignition to show both the letting go of the past as the trailer burns and the embodiment of the past in the present as Victor starts the engine of his father's pickup. In a sense, he is ready to be an Indian in the twentieth century without being consumed by the flames of resentment and anger, ready both to let his father go and to accept his connection to him. Once again, we see the different notion of time in American Indian cultures. To let his father go is not to leave him behind in some linear way, but ultimately to draw closer to him in his acceptance of what his father has bequeathed him. As Luci Tapahonso points out, we are who we are because the people who lived before us suffered and endured. To understand that is both to live in the present and to know that the past lives in us.

Having claimed his heritage, Victor can now share his father with Thomas without bitterness. When they arrive in front of Thomas's house back on the reservation, Victor pours half of his father's ashes into the jar in which Thomas has carried his money. As they talk, we learn that both boys are planning to take the ashes to the bridge over the Spokane River. Thomas puts his plan into typically spiritual terms, telling Victor that his father will "rise like a salmon" from the river. For Victor, on the other hand, scattering the ashes will be more like "cleaning out the attic." Lest this response (one of only a handful of lines retained from the original version of the story) make us doubt Victor's acceptance of his father, however, the film provides a last parallel. When Thomas asks Victor if he knows why Arnold Joseph left, alluding to the cause of the fire, Victor echoes his father's words from the beginning of the film: "He didn't mean to, Thomas." Thomas's nod and smile show that he recognizes Victor's forgiveness of his father, the forgiveness he has been working for throughout the journey.

We see the importance of Thomas's stories to Victor's healing process through Alexie's use of another repeated image. Thomas's favorite story about Arnold Joseph tells of the time Arnold took him to Denny's. Told by a dream to go to Spokane in order to receive a vision, Thomas hikes into the city and waits for his vision on the bridge over the Spokane River. Arnold sees him there and tells him that all he will get is mugged; then he takes him to breakfast. As Thomas tells the story, we see the scene from the past: Arnold reaches down to help the young boy to his feet. In the film's present, we see Victor's resentment, his look of pure hatred as Thomas savors the memory of his Denny's "Grand Slam" breakfast with Arnold, which represents the kind of moment that was rare in Victor's own relationship with his father. Later, when Victor collapses at the end of his run for help, the image of Arnold reaching down to help the boy up is repeated, but this time it is Victor he is reaching toward. In this wonderfully resonant image, Alexie's screenplay implies that Victor has now become part of Thomas's story, and in doing so he has finally found the ability to reconcile with and accept his father. As in "Yellow Woman," we are reminded that stories shape our journey, that we live the stories and become our own versions of them. Indeed, in an interview just before *Smoke Signals* was released, Alexie pointed out that Thomas's storytelling is really the center of the film, although that approach is cinematically unusual: "We sort of subvert the whole convention of 'show, not tell' and he's sort of 'tell it.'" Thomas's storytelling, Alexie adds, "is really the wheel that keeps the movie rolling."[17]

It is also clear that in finding the voice of Thomas as a center for the film, Alexie found a way to deepen immensely the brief story in *The Lone Ranger and Tonto* that became *Smoke Signals*. Adding the fire, which kills Thomas's parents, links Thomas to Victor and Arnold, and makes Thomas more central to the narrative, also provides the fire and ash imagery, which is introduced in Thomas's voice in the opening scenes and which, as we have seen, unifies the film. Victor's burning bitterness is more fully developed in the film, and Thomas becomes more important as his stories become the foil to that bitterness. It is as if Alexie discovered fully the deeper possibilities in the name Phoenix as he moved Thomas to the center of the narrative.

It is fitting that Alexie attributes the changed perspective in *Smoke Signals* to his own process of healing. In an interview with Dennis West and Joan M. West, Alexie says that his progress toward recovering from alcoholism has deeply affected his work:

> As I've been in recovery over the years and stayed sober, you'll see the work gradually freeing itself of alcoholism and going much deeper, exploring the emotional, sociological, and psychological reasons for any kind of addiction or dysfunctions within the community. I'm looking for the causes now, rather than the effects, and I think that's what Smoke Signals is about. The Lone Ranger and Tonto is about the effects of alcoholism on its characters, and I think the adaptation, Smoke Signals, is more about the causes of that behavior. It's more of a whole journey, you get there and you get back.[18]

As the quotation suggests, Alexie's own journey has led him to explore more deeply the journeys in which his characters participate. This double journey thus offers a fitting way to wrap up a course that has focused on the spiritual significance of the journey.

Alexie and *Smoke Signals* director Chris Eyre also add another dimension to the story and underscore a link with Silko's view when they use what Alexie calls "magic cuts" in the film's flashbacks. Each time the narrative goes to the past, a younger version of the character emerges through a door that the older version of the character had been approaching in the previous cut. Asked about that technique, Alexie responds in a way that underscores his connection to the traditions Silko refers to: "The way time works in Indian culture is more circular," he says. "There's a lot more culture on the screen than time."[19] As in "Yellow Woman," the past is not behind us as one point in a series of events; rather, it is with us every time we walk through a door or tell a story.

Including "Yellow Woman" and *Smoke Signals* in a world literature class, I would suggest, might enable us to accomplish several things. We can give students a sense of the cultural differences among American Indian peoples while showing them important similarities. We can explore the way in which the journey metaphor reaches across cultures and thereby show underlying human connections. We can also highlight differences in the ways in which the journey is described and call attention to the cultural values that underlie those differences. Most importantly, though, we can suggest to students that, to use Silko's words in *Ceremony*, stories "aren't just entertainment." By knowing about stories, we can become aware of the patterns we live and thus deepen and enrich our own journey.

Chapter 7

Out of the Classroom and into the Canyons: An American Indian Travel Course in Theory and Practice

The Problem of the Classroom

We are generally unaware of many of the ways in which we teach. This is probably inevitable: A dominant society cannot help but impose its assumptions about the world on its own members and on the members of other cultures in ways that are not necessarily conscious. The very structures we encounter in everyday life can reinforce those assumptions and yet become so familiar that we fail to notice the lesson. University campuses are especially important among silent teaching structures. As David Orr puts it in *The Nature of Design*, "buildings and landscape reflect a hidden curriculum that powerfully influences the learning process."[1] If we apply this truth to the way in which we study American Indian Literatures and cultures, we can see that several troubling assumptions are present in the very spaces in which the studying occurs.

At the beginning of my American and American Indian literature courses, for example, I ask students to look at the room we are sitting in: "Imagine that you're anthropologists from Mars," I say. "What cultural assumptions about the world in general and about education in particular can you find here?" At first they are not sure what I am talking about, since they have not been trained to look for cultural assumptions in architecture or any other of the many familiar structures among which we live and move, but as they catch on, they begin to see that most of what they have experienced as education is built into the room. First, of course, is the unexamined assumption that education happens indoors. I remember leaving my son at his afternoon kindergarten class and noting the energy of the children as they played outside before classes began. It was clear that in their running and tree climbing, their chasing and wrestling they were learning a great deal, but it was not sanctioned learning. That physical energy had to be contained within the indoor space of the classroom and converted to intellectual energy for it to count as real education. I felt sorry for the teachers who had to deal with that energy but even more sorry for the children who were getting the message that education means denying the sheer physical joy of being outside. At the age when children are most fully exploring their physical selves and their relation to the natural world, we put them in chairs and say, "Sit down; be still; be quiet." When they cannot, we categorize them as being unruly or even as suffering from disorders. Is it any wonder that we are struggling with adolescents who spend all their time in front of video screens when we teach them at an early age that only indoor mental activity has real social meaning? Even "physical education" has been reduced to a course or two in an entire high school or college career, and the real resources go into producing specialized athletes who learn much about competition and "winning" and very little about the joy of being embodied.

 As we move inside, the shape and arrangement of the room also tell us a great deal. They say that knowledge is something the teacher possesses and the students will receive. If they want to see another student who has something to say, they have to fight against the linear, rectangular layout. Thus, certain assumptions about authority are part of the very spaces we come to associate with education. The desks also reinforce the idea that bodies do not count—education is purely intellectual, and we have to be more or less immobilized in order to participate. The gray, unadorned walls and the windows (which are at the back of the rooms I teach in) say that learning is serious (and probably boring) and can take place only in the absence of "distractions" such as varied colors and natural phenomena—grass, trees, sky. Learning is divorced from place—what we are doing could be done equally well if we were in a similar space a thousand miles away—and of course, similar discussions *are* going on in similarly disconnected spaces even as we speak.

I point out to students that the average classroom full of Americans has a comfort range of approximately four degrees Fahrenheit: If the temperature is below seventy-two some students will be shivering and reaching for sweaters; if it is above seventy-six, some will begin fanning themselves. The presence of the heating and cooling unit affirms that this is the way things should be, even if the unit seldom works well in practice. If we are comfortable with the temperature we can forget about bodies and be minds—the "thinkers" that Descartes (and Western culture) tell us we are.

Above all, the room shows that we are a rectangle-making people. The room and virtually everything in it (except for the people) are rectangular. Concrete blocks, blackboards, books, paper, maps, desks, seating charts, calendars, laptop computers, the ubiquitous cell phones, everything proclaims that the rectangle, with its "right" angles is the "cor*rect*" shape, and if something is not right we will *rect*ify it. The word "right," and the root "rect" originally come from Indo-European "*riht*" meaning "straight," and "rich" comes from the same root. Our assumptions are obvious here: straight, right, correct, erect, rich—these words and the concepts they spring from define what we value.

Going outside does not change things much. If we examine the European American approach to land we see that the rectangle-making propensity governs our view of what is around us. We map land using latitude and longitude, imposing rectangles on an earth whose sphericity we are proud of having discovered. We divide areas of land into square sections, and then we arrange rectangular buildings into blocks. So the classroom is a microcosm of a created world filled with cultural assumptions about what is right and what needs to be corrected. Since the rectangle is extremely rare in nature, our maps, cities, and buildings (not to mention our calendars, paintings, books, and so on) proclaim our assumption that we need to impose our own order on a world that in our view is disorderly until we rearrange it.

Students will sometimes argue that rectangles are "efficient." They have a point, but only if we accept numerous assumptions about the nature of efficiency. For example, it is easier (and cheaper) to construct large buildings if they are rectangular. However, such an emphasis on size reflects once again our assumption that most activities should take place indoors; because we spend most of our time in buildings, they need to be large. Moreover, what we usually mean by "efficient" is, in fact, simply "cheaper," and this leaves us in the strange position of arguing that educational buildings are better if they are cheaper, whether or not they really accomplish very well the purpose of educating.

Bringing American Indian literature into such a space creates tensions that are obvious but not very convenient to acknowledge. The web of creation made by Spider Woman in Pueblo cultures is far removed from the linear and closed space of the classroom, which proclaims its disconnection from the world around. Though Pueblo and Hopi dwelling spaces are rectangular because of the materials and environment, the kivas or sacred spaces are often round. More importantly, the view of the world is one of cycles, of receiving and giving in a circular relationship, a relationship, not with "nature" (an abstract concept that reveals our culture's separation from what surrounds us), but with a particular place and all of its beings, both those that are animate and those that we cannot see moving. In Luci Tapahonso's poetry, for example, it is the sacred mountains that teach the people how to live, not a human authority in an intentionally isolated rectangle.

Thus the situation gets much trickier when we think more deeply about the issue of place as it is embodied in the classroom. Unlike the Hopi potter who prays over the clay before she digs it or the Pueblo builder who blesses the stone that will become part of a wall, we generally have no idea where the materials come from that went into the building that shelters us as we learn. Just outside Tucson, for example, one of two adjacent mountains that used to be called the "Twin Peaks" has been completely leveled to make Arizona Portland cement, and they are working pretty hard on the second twin. Is some of that mountain in the concrete blocks and mortar we are surrounded by here in Arkansas? That is not a relevant question in our curriculum. We do not generally know where the electricity comes from either, or who has been affected by its presence in our classroom. Was the uranium in the local nuclear plant mined on Pueblo or Navajo land by workers who might have developed cancer from exposure to the ore? Alternatively, does the power come from coal mined by the Peabody Company, which is rapidly depleting Navajo and Hopi water supplies? That is not part of what we study. Though the way in which the room might be connected to the land is not a conscious part of the curriculum, the absence of such knowledge or of any attempt to grapple with such topics definitely communicates information about what we consider important.

Moreover, the classroom is not simply separated from place; it is designed specifically to separate students from the places they come from and the places they live in. In American culture the classroom is generally seen as a kind of conduit—we step into it and become qualified to leave behind our former lives and embrace a success that rewards mobility, i.e., the ability and willingness to move anywhere in order to engage in our newly developed specialty. My own experience of leaving a farm outside Tucson to enter the University of Arizona and, after graduate school in Los Angeles, find a job in Arkansas, is fairly typical of the kind of "success" the classroom works for. In many ways, to enter the classroom is to embrace a way of seeing in which place becomes irrelevant. It educates us in the ability to live any place, which really means no place. Sunny Dooley, a Navajo storyteller, told me that she explained to her niece that there is a "strip monster," a mischief-making *yei*, who goes from city to city with a long bundle like a rolled-up carpet containing all the fast food outlets and strip malls that we see everywhere. He rolls out a certain length of his bundle in each city, and that is the reason they all look the same. The strip monster's carpet is the no place we learn to live in.

Since American Indian cultures are so fully rooted in place, it is little wonder that European education with its system of boarding schools was seen as an excellent way to destroy those cultures. Leaders such as the Hopi Yukiuma, who resisted white education even at the cost of long prison sentences, saw that educators, however well intentioned, were working for the destruction of a way of life based on connections to the land and the beings on it. In Leslie Marmon Silko's *Ceremony,* teachers tell the Pueblo children, "don't let the people at home hold you back."[2] The message is clear and terribly destructive—in order to succeed, American culture demands the separation of the individual from the land and the traditions that have grown from it. Simon Ortiz calls American public school education "a severe and traumatic form of brainwashing,"[3] and in his introduction to *Speaking for the Generations*, he is particularly emphatic about the importance of land when it comes to identity, and not just the identity of American Indian peoples: "Land and people are interdependent. . . . They cannot be separated and delineated into singular entities."[4]

Thus, to bring American Indian literature into the space of the classroom is to create a disjunction. As David Orr points out in *The Nature of Design*, "The curriculum embedded into a building instructs as fully and as powerfully as any course taught in it." The university classroom teaches "that locality, knowing where you are, is unimportant." The ultimate result, Orr concludes, is "mindlessness," the assumption that place does not even need to be considered.[5]

This situation is further aggravated by our emphasis on "wireless" technology. It is not unusual to see students walking together across campus or sitting together in a classroom, each of them engaged in a conversation with people who are not present. Most teachers, I expect, have had to add a warning to their syllabi about using cell phones in class, and the increasingly common use of cell phones in restrooms sometimes creates a rather striking illustration of the disjunction between conversation and place, the extent to which we are not where we are. Now, having made the whole campus wireless, my university is determined to ensure that every freshman student has a laptop computer and uses it in class. Having had a few students bring their computers to class, I can see that this "laptop initiative" will create a disturbing situation when it has been fully implemented. Students do not want to bring books to class, since there is no room on the desk for an open book and a computer, and books are an added burden to a student who is lugging a laptop. Since the computer is made for calling up and storing information (or communicating with people who are not in the place you are), laptop-equipped students tend to type whatever I say instead of participating in discussion. When someone gives you a high-tech hammer, everything looks like a nail. On the other hand, it gives students an excellent way to "instant message" other students, both in and out of class. Some instructors insist that class discussions should take place in cyberspace, since that is what students are becoming accustomed to, and we are being offered stipends to change our classes to online courses. This represents the closing of an absurd circle. Once technology enabled us to speak to those who were far away as if they were near; now the computer enables us to be in the same room yet communicate as if we were miles apart, or to move the discussion out of a place entirely, so that even the relatively isolated space of the classroom itself becomes irrelevant, and we are seemingly separated from any place at all. The reality, of course, is rather different. As we communicate on those computers we are connected to all the mines the materials came from, the workers who labored at low wages to shape them, the landfills and foreign countries where those materials will wind up, and, quite often, the rivers and wells that will be polluted as the result of extracting the metals that can be reused. Those connections, however, are usually invisible to us, and we seem to live in a world composed entirely of human creations.

 A friend of mine recently gave to her composition class an article presenting evidence that the use of computers and the Internet makes students more isolated, instead of "connecting" them. She expected to have a lively debate about the accuracy of the article, but to her surprise, her students agreed completely with the writer's premise. One student added that it was not just the Internet: The whole college experience—the need to work in order to afford tuition, cell phones, computers, and the various other technological tools that are required in our society, the lack of interaction in and around classrooms, the homework done in solitude—was in itself isolating. Students apparently have little time to interact with each other, let alone to experience life outside the made environment of the city.

The result of this distance, as Silko suggests in *Ceremony*, is fear. Those who "grow away from the earth" fear the world, and "they destroy what they fear."[6] Each semester in World Literature, as we prepare to study the English Romantic poets, I offer my students extra credit for completing a simple exercise: They are to go somewhere outside, away from human activity if possible, without cell phones, recorded music, books, or writing tools. They are to sit there and just observe for one hour and then write down a page or so documenting their responses. Their reports are revealing and disturbing. Most of my students, it seems, are afraid of snakes, deer, bears (even when the place where they sit is the nature reserve on campus, which is within a hundred yards of a busy street), spiders, bees and other insects, the woods, germs, sitting on the grass, strangers, students of other races, each other, and so on. One student even asked if there was any way she could somehow complete the assignment inside a building.

The Quaker educator Parker Palmer says that much of what passes for education in our schools is "death-dealing"— "a process that dissects life and distances us from the world because it is so deeply rooted in fear."[7] My students' responses to the exercise affirm his view. Jane Tompkins suggests a mechanism by which another kind of fear is transmitted from teacher to student. The teacher has learned to be afraid of failing to perform in the ways the educational system values, and she subconsciously communicates that fear of disapproval to her students: "Insofar as I was afraid to be exposed; they too would be afraid."[8] The rectangular classroom, with its linear and hierarchical arrangement of the world, walls us off from beings around us and demands our conformity to the correct way of conducting education.

In short, discussing American Indian literature in the educational space created by our culture is a bit like discussing the value of silence with the stereo blasting away—it can be done, but you have to wonder if there is a better way.

Beyond the Rectangle

For David Orr the solution lies in redesigning buildings to demonstrate and honor their connectedness with place. No doubt, students would be more open to the values of American Indian literature (and of most American literature) if the buildings in which they attend class were consciously and visibly designed with their connection to the local area in mind. Having grown up in Arizona, however, I have come to believe that students could be missing much of what is at stake in the works of writers such as Leslie Marmon Silko, Simon Ortiz, Ofelia Zepeda, and Luci Tapahonso if they stay in an Arkansas classroom, no matter how well designed it is. One glimpse of Mount Taylor from the Laguna or Acoma Pueblo, within the right context, might do more to promote understanding, it seemed to me, than hours of classroom lecture or discussion ever could.

However, "the right context" is not a simple thing. To take a tour of Acoma Sky City, visit some ruins, and hike or ride into Canyon De Chelly, might just be exchanging the box of the classroom experience for a boxful of tourist experiences—a collection of postcards and pictures, a pot, some jewelry, a kachina doll. I think we need to highlight and challenge more directly the students' assumptions about place, connectedness, and education. So as I set up a travel seminar for the first time I decided to begin with an examination of our way of living in a context that would throw students off balance and make them discover their own assumptions in a basic way. We went to the educational center run by a well know and highly respected organization called Heifer International and began with the "global village experience" in which students spend an afternoon working in an organic garden and then have to live for the evening and night in the kind of dwelling space they would find in Guatemala, Africa, Thailand, the Appalachians, or a Mexico City "barrio." They had to figure out a way to get water and firewood, to enhance their meager allowance of food by trading materials or labor with neighbors, to cook using a wood burning stove if they were "rich" by world standards, or an open fire and an automobile grille if they were less prosperous. In 2006, we expanded this part of the course by taking advantage of an extended version of the global village experience. Students spent three days and four nights in simple shelters, caring for gardens and animals, using proceeds from their labors to buy supplies in an international marketplace and finding that prices were higher for some citizens than for others. Some had to decide whether they would use their meager resources to help other groups who had less, and others had to take on the role of poorly paid laborer for their peers who had more. Coming off those experiences, students have a clearer sense of the meaning of shelter, food, fuel, and water as elements of a place, and they are ready to discuss our way of life more intensely. We raise questions about what it means to define ourselves as "consumers," the impact we have on other cultures because of that definition, the effect of our actions on the land and the beings we share it with. Also in 2006, Sara Groe, a UCA instructor who has studied problems associated with diet and the loss of traditional foods, raised questions about those connections as part of the course. At the same time, in order to show that there really are alternative and well developed views around, we look at different ways of defining our relationship to the land—Christian, Buddhist, and of course American Indian.

Meanwhile, students are reading literature and works about American Indian cultures. I developed the course with the help of Elaine Fox, a Sociology professor who has spent significant time as a nurse on the Navajo reservation, and she contributes to the pre-trip discussions so that we can get beyond the boxes of the "disciplines" as well, to show that literature and culture are connected and have to be understood together. She gives presentations on Navajo and Hopi cultures before the global village experience, so our discussions have an intellectual foundation as well as the hands-on component. I have provided a reading list at the end of this chapter, so I will focus here on just how the readings fit together. Chapter 6, "The Circle and the Square," from *Lame Deer, Seeker of Visions* by John Lame Deer and Richard Erdoes, gives students an introduction to some important aspects of American Indian culture, and, just as importantly, an engaging and challenging critique of European American culture. Then we focus more specifically on the cultures who live in the places we will visit. We have read Simon Ortiz's *Men on the Moon, Blue Horses Rush In* by Lucy Tapahonso, George Webb's *A Pima Remembers*, and Leslie Marmon Silko's *Ceremony*. I added selections from the Tohono O'odham poet Ofelia Zepeda's *Ocean Power* and the Hopi artist and poet Michael Kabotie's *Migration Tears* to the 2006 reading list. We also look at selected works that comment on the cultures and the issues involved in cultural conflict—John Loftin's introduction to Hopi religion, "Interior and Exterior Landscapes: The Pueblo Migration Stories" by Silko, and "Our Homeland, A National Sacrifice Area," from *Woven Stone* by Ortiz. We have reviewed different perspectives on the Navajo-Hopi land dispute, as well, which can readily be found online. (For example, "Beyond the Sacred Mountains: Effects of the Navajo-Hopi Land Dispute," Paula Giese, "Navajo-Hopi Land Dispute," and "The Hopi Tribe: Tutsqua Ancestral Land.) We wait to do the discussion of specific texts until we are on site, but the literature serves as a background for our discussion of cultural perspectives.

We also talk about the difference between being a tourist and being an informed guest or maybe even a pilgrim. I try to show students that we are not going as consumers—the trip is not about collecting experiences and souvenirs. I especially stress that we are going to give as well as receive—our money to help a Navajo guide, a Hopi educator, an Acoma family living on the reservation, our informed listening, our respect and willingness to learn, and our labor.

Then, after a day spent learning about tents, camp stoves, and camping skills in general, we head west. Our time on the road has expanded over the years. The first trip lasted ten days; the second year it was expanded to thirteen days; in 2004 we took fifteen days, which seems about right. I have provided a sample itinerary for the fifteen-day trip at the end of this chapter. We sleep in the tent or outside and cook our own meals, reflecting on where the food comes from and the significance of our use of it. We tour Acoma Sky City–our one "touristy" activity–since it serves as a good introduction not only to the Pueblo country and the setting of *Ceremony*, but also to the dilemma that faces those Native peoples who want to live in traditional ways in a world that makes that difficult. Our presence as visitors to the Acoma community clearly makes some of the people who live there uncomfortable—the students are acutely aware of the faces watching them from behind curtains as we go by—but our presence also helps the Acoma people live there instead of having to look for employment in the hostile world of Gallup or Grants, and our respectful appreciation of their way of life can perhaps help to alleviate the discomfort we bring. We make connections to *Ceremony*, discussing the importance of the speckled cattle as a way for Tayo to survive on the land and avoid the fate of the lost ones in Gallup, and to Simon Ortiz's poems in *Woven Stone* dealing with the way the loss of the land drove Acoma men to work for the railroad and the mines. We talk about the ways in which American Indian cultures have to adapt to the world we have brought, and we connect our discussion of that issue to Betonie's views of change in *Ceremony*.

After Acoma we hike into Canyon DeChelly with Dave Wilson, a Navajo guide who can discuss the historical and spiritual significance of the place; sometimes we also have an archaeologist from the Museum of Northern Arizona with us, and the juxtaposition of the two perspectives can be quite enlightening. Either before or after our time in the Canyon, we meet with Sunny Dooley, a Navajo storyteller who tells us about her culture and the role of stories in that culture and takes us on a walk along the rim of the canyon so we can see how stories arise from features of the landscape and are inseparable from places such as Spider Rock. I was able to contact these educators through the Museum of Northern Arizona, whose services have been invaluable in setting up the trips. We tour the Indian Health Services hospital in Chinle, which includes a hogan as part of its healing facilities, and if possible we meet with Johnson Dennison, the Navajo singer who is on staff at the hospital. The hospital staff is very helpful in setting up such meetings. Our experience at the hospital leads to an informed discussion of such things as the character of Betonie in *Ceremony* and Luci Tapahonso's poems.

The next phase of the trip takes us to the Hopi reservation, where we meet with a Hopi potter to learn the entire process of making a pot, from praying over the clay to firing the finished pot with sheep manure; we discuss such things as the significance of migration petroglyphs and pictographs, the fate of Awatovi, and the Hopi view of who they are and where they come from with our Hopi guide. We have a traditional meal with a family. Most importantly, we do a work project that enables us to give something back to our hosts. One time we plastered a house in the traditional Hopi way—using mud and our hands—so it could serve as part of a ceremony. Ray Coin, our Hopi guide that year, had already told us that the Hopi do their ceremonies for the healing of all people, not just the Hopi, and to participate in the coming ceremony in that way was particularly significant. In 2004 we worked on an orchard with a Hopi cultural educator and her mother (Susan and Dorothy Secakuku), pruning ancient trees that had been brought by the Spaniards and helping to clear the road to a spring that waters the orchard and the gardens where they are establishing native crops. We also have met with Michael Kabotie, a Hopi artist and poet who is using the style of traditional kiva art to tell his own stories about the American experience, and with Hopi elders who discussed their attempts to preserve tradition in the face of encroachment by mainstream American values. In 2004, we were fortunate enough to be on the Hopi reservation when a Corn Dance took place, so we attended with the Secakukus as our guides to the ceremony. Once again, these experiences were arranged with the help of the Museum of Northern Arizona.

Moving from the Colorado Plateau to the desert valleys, we have met with Ramona Button, a Pima (Akimel O'odham) woman who raises traditional crops, including corn for Hopi people who need to ensure the survival of their traditional varieties in the face of persistent drought. She and her husband Terry have brought together large numbers of the unworkable 40-acre allotments created by the Dawes Act, and they farm them very successfully and share the proceeds with the heirs of the original owners of the plots—sometimes over 100 to a single plot. Ramona joins us in a traditional Pima meal and talks to us about the significance of the corn, tepary beans, saguaro fruit, and squash we eat. In

2004 we met with Robert Stone, the manager of the community-owned Gila River Farms, and we discussed the Pima people's efforts to preserve and adapt their agricultural values; then we watched and listened as Robert sang for traditional dancers at the Gila River Cultural Center. I was able to set up these experiences through family connections in Arizona—my father and brother both live near the Gila River Reservation, and we have all worked on construction jobs with Pima people, who are generally very willing to share information about their efforts to preserve their land and traditional ways.

As we have these experiences we are also discussing the literature, talking about *Ceremony* in the shadow of Mount Taylor and with an awareness of the difficulty facing people whose culture is under constant pressure to become "American"; stopping to read Luci Tapahonso's poem about the sacred mountains, "This Is How They Were Placed for Us,"[9] as we approach the San Francisco Peaks; looking at the story of George Webb's life after we drive along the dry wash that the Gila River has become; exploring Simon Ortiz's depiction of "Mericanos" who learn from Pueblo people to see "the meaning of something,"[10] as we reflect on what our experiences have taught us. Though I have taught *Ceremony* more than a dozen times, no classroom discussion that I have ever led comes close to the talk we had under the cottonwood trees near Canyon De Chelly the day after we drove past Paguate and Cubero, talked to a jewelry maker near Old Laguna, visited the Acoma pueblo, and saw Enchanted Mesa from the desert near the place where the novel begins. Issues of cultural tension, land destruction, healing, and stories were alive for those students in ways they can never be in the classroom.

Just as importantly, the students are visibly changing along the way. On the second trip, for example, our big tent went up every night at first because the students were frightened of the desert—those snakes, spiders, and scorpions, and all that open space. Then one night the tent crew asked if they had to put it up. It stayed packed for the rest of the trip, as the students realized that their fears were groundless (pun intended). The importance and significance of water becomes very real to students who have to carry and heat it in order to wash dishes, who go several days without the luxury of a shower, and who sometimes have to learn at first hand what happens to hikers in the desert who do not carry enough. Food also takes on new significance: When I offered to stop at a restaurant near the end of the second trip there was rebellion—cooking food together was no longer a chore; it had become a ceremony that the students did not want to miss. The view of shelter also changed. We spent a night at my father's house on the edge of the Gila River reservation south of Phoenix, and everyone quickly moved outside without even discussing it, no longer quite as comfortable within the air-conditioned space that used to be home. The students develop a deeper understanding of and respect for the cultures and the people they encounter, and a deeper awareness about their own lives and assumptions.

Potholes

Of course the road is not completely smooth. Our adventures with water might help to illustrate the kinds of tension that can arise. On the first trip, I noticed that there was a huge collection of plastic water bottles, as students felt they had to buy something at every stop and could not do without the familiar taste and coldness of bottled water. They thought that recycling the bottles made it just fine, but recycling bins are few and far between in the Arizona desert, so we quickly had bottles taking up nearly as much space in the vans as people. Moreover, the Hopi are proud of their water and have had to fight against those who want to bottle and sell it, and the students' suspicion of its slightly effervescent qualities, and their insistence on finding sources of bottled water, led to some tension. The water situation resulted in a fruitful discussion, though, and before the second trip I talked about water and the significance and cost to the land of drinking it refrigerated from plastic bottles, as opposed to drinking the water that our hosts drink.

On the other hand, it is also hard to convince some students that they really do need to drink that much water and eat that many salty snacks when we hike in the desert. It sometimes takes the first bout of nausea and headache to make a student respect the sun and the six- to seven-thousand-foot altitude, which is very different from the air-conditioned classroom. There have been minor squabbles, people who do not quite get along at first, but those seem to smooth out. It is often hard to work enough discussion time and time for reflection into the schedule, and students affected by altitude and sun can get tired and cranky as we move from place to place.

Another difficulty resulted from my assumption that students would know how to put up a tent and use a camp stove, or at least be able to read instructions for putting up a tent and using a camp stove. The first night of the first trip we arrived at Palo Duro Canyon State Park at about six o'clock in the evening with plenty of daylight left, and after a prolonged struggle, we finally ate our evening meal in the dark three hours later. Now I spend half a day having an assigned tent crew put up the tents, take them down and pack them, and then demonstrate to the rest of the students how it is done. Each student then takes a turn lighting the Coleman stove. I also learned that it is crucial to assign each student to a team with a specific task (e.g., loading the vans, handling the tents, doing a final check of the campground before we leave, and so on), to arrange a cooking rotation that gives everyone a turn, and to ensure that everyone works according to a carefully arranged schedule. On a travel day, for example, belongings must be out of the tents and ready for the van loaders before anyone gets breakfast. If this kind of scheduling is not done, the non-traditional women students (or the teachers if there are no older women students) will wind up doing all the cooking, cleaning up, and packing. When that happened on the first trip, it became an important "teachable moment," an opportunity to discuss the role of women in our culture and the anger that can stem from the way others assume they will fill that role.

Then there is the trip home. I have come to realize that the interstate highway system is a powerful cultural corridor. That strip of concrete, billboards, and speeding vehicles silently reinforces certain assumptions about our relationship to the world just as powerfully as the university classroom and campus do. Students who have begun taking time for activity and reflection and have practiced bringing awareness to eating, drinking, and buying, can suddenly become impatient, full-fledged consumers when we hit I-40. Hamburgers, french fries, ice cream, Coke, and cries of "Let's just get home" and "Why can't you drive over seventy?" can threaten to smother the discussion. So we get together and talk about how to bring the journey home.

Completing the Circle

The classic journey story—present in so many cultures—begins with the traveler living an ordinary life in the terms of society until some circumstance propels him or her into an alternate world. In this world things have heightened significance, and the traveler is transformed in the encounter with this new significance. The return to the everyday world is usually perilous: The transformation has made it difficult for the traveler to come back to the old life and incorporate the newly gained knowledge. The traveler must acknowledge and embody his or her transformation—the real story of the journey—and yet also come back to live in the world she or he left. It is hard to come back after the transformation the journey demands without either abandoning the new knowledge or finding oneself cut off from what used to be home. The familiar world we left has not changed, yet the lessons of the journey have changed our relationship to it, and that can make the traveler's life difficult.

The students who go on the Southwest seminar trip face several difficulties. Some of them are minor—a few students say they have a hard time sleeping in a bed again. There are tearful farewells as the bonds created on the trip are broken by the return to student life and its demands on time. Participants complain that they cannot talk about the trip to their friends in Conway because it is impossible to communicate what it was like to someone who was not there. Perhaps the hardest question posed by our return, though, is how to bring what we have learned back to Conway, Arkansas. Students have responded in different ways: Some have decided on career changes, and others seem to return to the old life without great difficulty, though they often tell me that they think of the trip nearly every day.

After one trip, a "non-traditional" student asked me for ways of doing something different in Conway, and, since I had recently read a couple of articles on community gardens, I suggested that she look into that possibility. She was the kind of student to whom one should not make casual remarks. Within two weeks we had an appointment with the mayor of Conway, and, to make a long story short, we soon had land, water, and the help of the city director of parks and recreation. The garden has grown slowly and not always smoothly, but it has become an outdoor classroom as well as a place for local people to grow vegetables. Another student who went on the trip got the honors college to sponsor an organic gardening class, which was offered unofficially at first (with me as spare-time teacher) but can now be taken for credit. Students discuss theory and practice in the classroom, but they also spend several afternoons and weekends with their hands in the soil. Among the works they read are descriptions of planting from an American Indian perspective, of course. The course has turned out to be one of the most popular honors seminars, and several students have taken plots in the garden to continue growing vegetables after the course has ended. I have also had several interns from Hendrix College, a private liberal arts college across town, who have worked with me in the garden and gotten grants to help develop it, an arrangement that began when some Hendrix students went on the Southwest trip.

On the face of it, it seems a long way from Canyon De Chelly, the Hopi mesas, and the fields of the Pima people to a garden in Conway. It all fits together, though, I think. Contemporary American Indian literature calls not just for literary appreciation but for action—new ways of connecting. If we simply become indignant about the treatment of the people and the land without changing the way we relate to them, then our education, I think, has been largely futile. Ultimately, though we can learn a great deal from the Pueblo, the Navajo, the Hopi, and the Pima peoples, we cannot look to them to solve the problem of our disconnectedness. Really getting beyond the classroom with its linear order and isolation from other beings means finding alternative ways of connecting here, in the places where we live day to day. We have to learn how to live on and with the land where we find ourselves. Fortunately, once students do get out, they do not go back in all that easily. It is quite fitting, I think, that students who come back from visiting the canyons have helped other students get out of the classroom and into the garden.

Nuts and Bolts

Anyone who wants to plan a travel course such as the one I have described first needs to establish connections, of course. Without a lot of work ahead of time, a group may run the risk of offending local people or being relegated to tourist spots. As I mentioned earlier, I have been fortunate in having a colleague, Dr. Elaine Fox, who has worked as both sociologist and nurse on the Navajo Reservation and is informed about and appreciative of Navajo and Hopi traditions. It was her experience that encouraged me to make the attempt in the first place. We made an exploratory trip nearly a year before the first travel seminar took place. I had contacted faculty at Northern Arizona University as well, and they recommended talking to the Museum of Northern Arizona. The museum staff was my second stroke of good fortune: Tracy Anderson, who was the head of the Ventures programs and has since been promoted to director of educational programs, is knowledgeable, resourceful, very sensitive to cultural issues, and extremely adept at keeping students going under difficult conditions during the Colorado Plateau part of the trip. Her replacement in the Ventures program, Lisa Lamberson, was similarly competent and helpful. The other staff members the museum has provided have been highly qualified. Now that I have established friendships among the Hopi and Navajo guides we meet with, I have thought of setting up that part of the trip on my own, but I have decided against it because Tracy, Lisa, and the museum staff do such a competent and thoughtful job that the money they get is more than a bargain, and it goes to help an institution that does excellent work, supporting American Indian artists, bringing together representatives of the peoples of the Colorado Plateau, and educating the public about cultural issues.

Funding is also a tricky consideration, since student budgets are limited. Fortunately, the nature of the course contributes to keeping expenses down. Since we camp every night, our housing expenses range from a high of twenty-four dollars for the whole group (Palo Duro Canyon State Park and the Desert View campground in Grand Canyon National Park) to free (Canyon De Chelly, the Hopi Reservation, the area around my brother's house in central Arizona). By doing our own cooking we save lots of money as well. I ask each student to give me $150 (ten dollars a day) for food, camping, and other expenses. In the past I have been able to return some of it at the end of the trip, though rising costs have led me to plan to budget twelve dollars a day in the future.

As I mentioned before, the Museum of Northern Arizona contracts with our Navajo and Hopi educators, and the museum staff will work within the budget I give them. Grand Canyon National Park—and other parks—will grant a fee waiver to groups visiting for educational purposes. A letter to the appropriate office and some documentation of course content and university accreditation is all it takes.

We take university vans and divide the rental and gas costs. To make a long story short, students going on the trip in the summer of 2006 paid about $1700 for all expenses—tuition and fees for three hours' course credit, travel, food, camping, and all programming. This compares quite favorably with other travel courses, which usually involve airline fares and motel charges. Of course, the success of the course depends on finding enough students who are willing to "rough it," but that is what the experience is all about anyway—getting back in touch with the land, with the real source of food, shelter, and life.

To be blunt, I do not get much real support from the university administration for this kind of course. Students have to rely on the usual sources of financial aid, and though the Dean of Liberal Arts encourages me to continue offering the course, there apparently is not much he can do in the way of helping students find extra funding—the major need I run into. However, that, I suppose, comes along with the nature of the course: If you want to get out of the box, you cannot really expect the box makers to be a major source of support. The exception has been the Honors College, which does provide honors students with Travel Abroad Grants for the course (stretching the meaning of "abroad") and has been very helpful in many other ways. Generally, however, I find that students who really want to go find ways to manage it. In 2004, for instance, I did not have a single student who received extra funding.

In spite of my initial fears, I have not had problems with liability, because the university's insurance coverage extends to students participating in official university activities. As long as the proper papers are filled out at the right time, I am assured that we are covered in that area. Of course, I think it is important to be reasonably well versed in the kind of terrain to which we are going. My own experience hiking and camping in the Southwest has taught me to be attentive to students' physical condition and to keep both eyes open for signs of dehydration or altitude sickness. The students joke that I have only one response to any situation—"drink some water; eat something salty."

This course takes much more work than anything else I do. I am still dealing with some problems and issues—I want to connect with Navajo students at Diné College in Tsaile, and possibly meet with Ofelia Zepeda in Tucson, for example, and I have not entirely figured out how to make the road home something other than an endurance test. As I write this, I am preparing to travel to Arizona to set up the activities we will participate in when we go the next time, and I am working to bring Sunny Dooley to campus so students can get a sense of the Navajo traditions, people, and culture we will encounter on the trip. By May of next year I know I will be questioning my sanity, having struggled with the university administration over details that do not fit into their administrative rectangles, having had students drop out at the last minute, thinking about the planning and grocery shopping and possibilities for disaster I have left to face. Nevertheless, I also know that when we return in June I'll be ready to go again. It is that kind of experience.

Soutwest Travel Seminar: A Sample Reading List

"Beyond the Sacred Mountains: Effects of the Navajo-Hopi Land Dispute." 1997.
    21 May 2006 <http//xroads.virginia.edu/~MA97/dinetah/dispute.html.>
Giese, Paula. "Navajo-Hopi Land Dispute." 20 March 1997. 21 May 2006
    <www.kstrom.net/isk/maps/az/navhopi.html>.
"The Hopi Tribe: Tutsqua Ancestral Land," 2006. 21 May 2006 <www.**hopi**.nsn.us/
    ancestral_**land**.asp>.
Kabotie, Michael (Lomawywesa). *Migration Tears*. Los Angeles: American Indian

Studies Center, 1987.

Lame Deer, John (Fire) and Richard Erdoes. *Lame Deer, Seeker of Visions.* New York: Touchstone, 1973.

Loftin, John. "A Religious Practicality." *Religion and Hopi Life in the Twentieth Century.* 3–13.

Ortiz, Simon. *Woven Stone.* Tucson: University of Arizona Press, 1992.

———. "Hiding, West of Here." *Men on the Moon: Collected Short Stories.* Tucson: University of ArizonaPress, 1999. 191–96.

Silko, Leslie Marmon. *Ceremony.* 1977. New York: Penguin, 1986.

———. "Interior and Exterior Landscapes: The Pueblo Migration Stories." *Yellow Woman and a Beauty of the Spirit: Essays on Native American Life Today.* New York: Simon and Schuster, 1997. 25–47.

Zepeda, Ofelia. *Ocean Power: Poems from the Desert.* Tucson: University of Arizona Press, 1995.

Southest Travel Seminar: A Sample Itinerary (2006)

June 5 Heifer Ranch orientation on UCA campus— Time and room TBA

June 6-9: Heifer International Global Village.

June 11: Departure and the long drive. We will camp at Palo Duro State Park south of Amarillo, Texas.

June 12: Drive via Albuquerque, New Mexico, to Acoma Pueblo for a tour of Sky City at 2:30 p.m.; Camp at Bluewater State Park, New Mexico.

June 13: Drive to Chinle, Arizona, meet with Don Keller, MNA educator, Sunny Dooley, Navajo storyteller; camp at Canyon De Chelly National Monument, Cottonwood Campground.

June 14: Guided overnight hike into Canyon de Chelly with Don Keller and Dave Wilson, Navajo educator and guide, who will tell us about the significance of the place for the Navajo people and culture. Camp in Canyon De Chelly.

June 15: Morning—Hike out, then break for journals, discussion, rest. Visit the Navajo Health Services Hospital in the afternoon (3 p.m.). Camp at Canyon De Chelly.

June 16: Leave for the Hopi Reservation. *Note: Photography, sketching, and recording of any kind (video, audio, etc.) are strictly prohibited on the Hopi reservation.* Meet Susan Secakaku, Hopi educator; Piki demonstration; begin work on service-learning project. Camp at the Secakaku farm and orchard.

June 17: Morning–Hopi ceremony (if possible). Afternoon: conclude service-learning project (farm work and traditional cooking workshop); traditional Hopi meal.

June 18: Morning—leave for Grand Canyon; afternoon— hike into Grand Canyon; Camp at Desert View campground.

June 19: Leave for Museum of Northern Arizona in Flagstaff. Lunch at Hart Prairie. Evening—free time, showers, laundry, discussion. Camp on MNA grounds. *Note: Smoking is prohibited on the Museum grounds.*

June 20: Morning—tour museum; meet with Michael Kabotie for a discussion of traditional and contemporary Hopi art; tour collections. Afternoon—cultural discussion: Navajo and Hopi cultures. Camp on Museum grounds.

June 21: Leave Flagstaff—an easy day for sleeping in, reflection, catching up on journals, discussion. We'll enjoy Oak Creek Canyon and the

Sedona area, tour Montezuma Castle. Camping in Queen Creek.

June 22: Early morning hike in the San Tan Mountains. Visit Gila River Farms (Pima tribe); evening session with Pima storyteller. Camping at the Shumaker house.

June 23: Travel through Salt River Canyon, the White River Apache Reservation, the White Mountains. Camp at Datil Wells Recreation Site, New Mexico.

June 24: Continue trip; camp at Foss State Park, Oklahoma.

June 25: Back to Conway.

June 27: Post-trip discussion TBA

Notes

Chapter 1: Learning from Literature

1. We can see one symptom of the problems this book deals with in our failure to agree on what to call ourselves or the indigenous peoples of this land. I realize that to call ourselves "Americans" is in a sense to usurp title to the whole place, to ignore that there are many other peoples on the continents of North and South America. At the same time, "America" is first and foremost an idea (or a set of ideas), and "European Americans," as I use the term here, refers to those of us who share a heritage of European culture (including, in many ways, African Americans) and have been taught to subscribe more or less to the ideas and assumptions included in that construction we call "America." I have also used the term "American Indian" to refer to the indigenous peoples of North America when the individual cultural term (Hopi, Navajo or Diné, Pima or Akimel O'Odham, etc.) is not appropriate: that term seems to work better than "Native American," since traditional Navajo, Hopi, and other peoples generally do not subscribe to the set of values that are included in the noun "American." In my experience, they call themselves "Indians," usually with a certain amount of humor. "North American Indians" would be better, perhaps, though unwieldy.
2. Wendell Berry, *The Unsettling of America: Culture and Agriculture* (San Francisco: Sierra Club, 1977), 4.
3. Leslie Marmon Silko, *Ceremony* (New York: Penguin, 1977), 191.
4. Simon Ortiz, *Woven Stone* (Tucson: University of Arizona Press, 1992), 360.
5. Jeff Berglund, "'Planting the Seeds of Revolution': An Interview with Poet Esther Belin (Diné)," *Studies in American Indian Literatures* Ser.2, 17 (Spring 2005): 66.
6. Andrea M. Penner, "The Moon Is So Far Away: An Interview with Luci Tapahonso," *Studies in American Indian Literature* Ser. 2, 8 (1996): 9.
7. *Woven Stone*, 14.
8. Susan Berry Brill De Ramirez, "Introduction: 'A Spring Wind Rising ... Listen. You Can Hear It,'" *Studies in American Indian Literature* Ser. 2, 16 (2004): 3.
9. Diane Glancy, "He Has More Than One Ear," *Studies in American Indian Literature* Ser. 2, 7 (1995): 1.
10. Glancy, 2.

Chapter 2: Beginnings

1. Sherman Alexie, *Indian Killer* (New York: Warner Books, 1996), 84.
2. Simon Ortiz, *Woven Stone* (Tucson: University of Arizona Press, 1992), 93.
3. Ortiz, 347.
4. Ortiz, 348.
5. Ortiz, 8.
6. Ortiz, 319
7. Ortiz, 297.
8. Ortiz, 360.
9. Ortiz, 363.
10. Simon Ortiz, "To Change Life in a Good Way," *Men on the Moon* (Tucson: University of Arizona Press, 1999), 113.
11. Ortiz, "To Change Life," 113.
12. Ortiz, "To Change Life," 114.
13. Ortiz, "To Change Life," 115.
14. Ortiz, "To Change Life, 116.
15. Ortiz, "Hiding, West of Here," *Men on the Moon*, 194.
16. Ortiz, "Hiding," 195.
17. Ortiz, "Hiding," 196.
18. Ortiz, *Woven Stone*, 363.

Chapter 3: Putting a World Together

1. Virginia Kennedy, "Unlearning the Legacy of Conquest: Possibilities for *Ceremony* in the Non-Native Classroom," *American Indian Culture and Research Journal* 28 (2004): 76.
2. Silko, Leslie Marmon. *Ceremony* (New York: Viking, 1977), 4.
3. Silko, 34–35.
4. Helen Jaskoski, "Thinking Woman's Children and the Bomb," *Explorations in Ethnic Studies* 13 (July, 1990): 5.
5. Silko, *Ceremony,* 125.
6. Silko, 126.
7. Silko, 68.
8. Silko, 74.
9. Silko, 51.
10. Silko, 195.
11. Silko, 135.
12. Silko, 191.
13. Silko, 204.
14. Louis Owens, *Other Destinies: Understanding the American Indian Novel* (Norman: University of Oklahoma Press, 1992), 187.

15. Silko, 94.
16. Ibid.
17. Silko, 182.
18. Silko, 95.
19. Silko, 96.
20. Silko, 98–99.
21. Silko, 181.
22. Silko, 99.
23. Silko, 181.
24. Silko, 222.
25. Silko, 223.
26. Silko, 104.
27. Silko, 74.
28. Silko, 77.
31. Silko, 246.
32. Silko, 247.
33. Robert M. Nelson, "Settling for Vision in Silko's *Ceremony*: Sun Man, Arrowboy, and Tayo," *American Indian Culture and Research Journal* 28 (2004): 67–73.
34. Silko, 253.
35. Silko, 257.
36. For an excellent discussion of this issue and references to the relevant articles, see Robert M. Nelson, "Rewriting Ethnography: The Embedded Texts in Leslie Silko's *Ceremony*," in *Telling the Stories: Essays on American Indian Literatures and Cultures*, ed. Elizabeth Hoffman Nelson and Malcolm A. Nelson.

Chapter 4: "Made of Prayers"

1. Herman Melville, "Bartleby the Scrivener," *The Piazza Tales and Other Prose Pieces* (Chicago: Northwestern University Press, 1987), 29.
2. Leslie Marmon Silko, *Ceremony* (New York: Penguin, 1977), 246.
3. Diane Glancy, "He Has More Than One Ear," *Studies in American Indian Literatures* Ser. 2, 7 (1995): 2.
4. Glancy, 1.
5. "The Weekend Is Over," *Sáanii Dahataał: The Women Are Singing* (Tucson: University of Arizona Press, 1993), 4.
6. "In 1864," *Sáanii Dahataał*, 10.
7. "The Weekend Is Over," 4.
8. "In Praise of Texas," *Blue Horses Rush In* (Tucson: University of Arizona, 1997), 11.
9. "One Dog Story," *Sáanii Dahataał*, 29–32.
10. "I Remembered This One in Tucson," *Blue Horses Rush In,* 57–59.
11. "One Dog Story," *Sáanii Dahataał*, 8.

12. Penner, "The Moon Is So Far Away," 11.
13. *Sáanii Dahataał*, 8.
14. Ibid.
15. *Sáanii Dahataał*, 10.
16. Ibid.
17. Ibid.
18. Ibid.
19. Penner, 8.
20. "A Birthday Poem," *Blue Horses Rush In* 79.
21. Ibid.
22. *Blue Horses Rush In*, 80.
23. Ibid.
24. *Blue Horses Rush In*, 15.
25. Ibid.
26. Penner, 10.
27. *Blue Horses Rush In*, 15–16.
28. *Blue Horses Rush In*, 16.
29. Ibid.
30. A very helpful online description of Navajo culture and mythology (including the Changing Woman stories) can be found in "Between Four Sacred Mountains: The Diné and the Land in Contemporary America," http://xroads.virginia.edu/~MA97/dinetah/front.html.
31. *Blue Horses Rush In*, 39.
32. *Blue Horses Rush In*, 40.
33. *Blue Horses Rush In*, 41.
34. *Blue Horses Rush In*, 42.
35. Alberto Rios, "Some Extensions on the Sovereignty of Science," *The Smallest Muscle in the Human Body* (Port Townsend, WA: Copper Canyon, 2002), 103.
36. See, for example, Alexis De Tocqueville's description of the American response to criticism in *Democracy in America*, ed. J. P. Mayer, trans. George Lawrence (Garden City, NY: Doubleday, 1966), 256: "But the power [of the majority] which dominates in the United States does not understand being mocked . . . . The least reproach offends it, and the slightest sting of truth turns it fierce . . . . Hence the majority lives in a perpetual state of self-adoration."
37. *Ceremony*, 68.

Chapter 5: The Quiet People

1. "Pima Stories of the Beginning of the World," *The Norton Anthology of AmericanLiterature*, ed. Nina Baym, et al., vol. A (New York: Norton, 2003), 25.
2. *The Norton Anthology of American Literature*, 27.
3. *The Norton Anthology of American Literature*, 28.

4. Anna Moore Shaw, *A Pima Past* (Tucson: University of Arizona Press, 1974), 162.
5. Kenneth Funsten, "100 Books for the Modern Person," *Los Angeles Times*, Sep. 20, 1981, Book Section, 3. "100 Books for the Modern Person by Kenneth Funsten (*Los Angeles Times*)," http://www.interleaves.org/~rteeter/grtlat.html.
6. George Webb, "Preface," *A Pima Remembers* (Tucson: University of Arizona Press, 1959), n. p.
7. Webb, 30.
8. Webb, 48.
9. Webb, 35.
10. Webb, 36.
11. Webb, 86.
12. Webb, 116.
13. Webb, 118.
14. Webb, 121.
15. Webb, 124–25.
16. Webb, 125–6.
17. Webb, 126.
18. Shaw, *A Pima Past*, 91.
19. Francine Ratner Kaufman, *Diabestiy: The Obesity-Diabetes Epidemic That Threatens America—And What We Must Do to Stop It* (New York: Bantam, 2005), 130.
20. Kaufman, 130.
21. Kaufman, 130.
22. Kaufman, 14.

Chapter 6: American Indian Literatures as World Literature

1. Leslie Marmon Silko, "Interior and Exterior Landscapes: The Pueblo Migration Stories," *Yellow Woman and a Beauty of the Spirit: Essays on American Life Today* (New York: Simon and Schuster, 1996), 27–28.
2. Patricia Clark Smith with Paula Gunn Allen, "Earthly Relations, Carnal Knowledge: Southwestern American Indian Writers and Landscape," *"Yellow Woman,"* ed. Melody Graulich (New Brunswick, NJ: Rutgers University, 1993), 118.
3. Leslie Marmon Silko, "Yellow Woman," *The Norton Anthology of World Literature*, 2nd edition, ed. Sarah Lawall, et al., vol. F (New York: Norton, 2002), 3147.
4. Anonymous, "The Bear Man," *The Portable North American Indian Reader*, ed. Frederick W. Turner III (New York: Penguin, 1977), 102–5. This book is now out of print, but similar versions of the story are available online; see http://firstpeople.us/FP_Html_Legends/TheBearMan_Cherokee.html. The story was originally published in James Mooney, *Myths of the Cherokee, 19th Annual Report of the Bureau of American Ethnology, 1897–98,* Part I (Washington, 1900).
5. "Interior and Exterior Landscapes," 26.

6. Silko, "Yellow Woman," 3146.
7. Silko, *Ceremony* (New York: Norton, 1977), 260.
8. Naguib Mahfouz, "Zaabalawi," *The Norton Anthology of World Literature,* 2nd edition, ed. Sarah Lawall et al., vol. F (New York: Norton, 2002), 2531.
9. Premchand (Dhanpat Rai Shrivastava), "Zaabalawi," *The Norton Anthology of World Literature,* 1916.
10. Smith and Allen, "Earthly Relations," 139.
11. *Yellow Woman and a Beauty of the Spirit,* 70.
12. "A Leslie Marmon Silko Interview," *Conversations with Leslie Marmon Silko,* ed. Ellen L. Arnold (Jackson: University of Mississippi Press, 2000), 77.
13. "Fifth World: The Return of Ma ah shra true ee, the Giant Serpent," *Yellow Woman and a Beauty of the Spirit,* 125.
14 "Yellow Woman and a Beauty of the Spirit," 72.
15. "An Interview with Leslie Marmon Silko," *Conversations with Leslie Marmon Silko,* 148–49.
16. "Yellow Woman," 3150.
17. Mike Jones, "This Is What it Means . . . : A Conversation with *Smoke Signals* writer Sherman Alexie," http://www.indiewire.com/people/int_Alexie_Sherman_980116.html, viewed on November 14, 2006.
18. Dennis West and Joan West, "Sending Cinematic Smoke Signals: And Interview with Sherman Alexie," *Cineaste* 23 (1998), 28–33; viewed online at http://www.lib.berkeley.edu/MRC/alexie.html March 8, 2006.
19. "This Is What It Means . . ."

Chapter 7: Out of the Classroom and into the Canyons

1. David W. Orr, *The Nature of Design: Ecology, Culture, and Human Intention.* (New York: Oxford University Press, 2002), 127–28.
2. Leslie Marmon Silko, *Ceremony* (New York: Penguin, 1986), 51.
3 Simon Ortiz, *Woven Stone* (Tucson: University of Arizona Press, 1992), 8.
4. Simon Ortiz, *Speaking for the Generations: Native Writers on Writing* (Tucson: University of Arizona Press, 1998), xii.
5. Orr, 128.
6. Silko, 135.
7. Parker J. Palmer, "The Grace of Great Things: Reclaiming the Sacred in Knowing, Teaching, and Learning," *The Heart of Learning: Spirituality in Education,* ed. Steven Glazer (New York: Tarcher/Penguin, 1999), 17.
8. Jane Tompkins, *A Life in School: What the Teacher Learned* (Reading, MA: Perseus, 1996), 119.
9. Luci Tapahonso, "This Is How They Were Placed For Us," *Blue Horses Rush In* (Tucson: University of Arizona Press, 1998), 39–42.
10. Simon Ortiz, "Hiding, West of Here," *Men on the Moon* (Tucson: University of Arizona Press, 1999), 196.

Works Cited

Alexie, Sherman. *Indian Killer.* New York: Warner Books, 1996.

Anonymous. "The Bear Man." *The Portable North American Indian Reader.* Ed. Frederick W. Turner, III. New York: Penguin, 1977. 102–105. http://firstpeople.us/FP_Html_Legends/TheBearMan_Cherokee.html.

Arnold, Ellen L., ed. *Conversations with Leslie Marmon Silko.* Jackson: University of Mississippi Press, 2000.

Baym Nina, et al., eds. "Pima Stories of the Beginning of the World." *The Norton Anthology of American Literature.* 7th ed. 5 vols. New York: Norton, 2003. 1: 21–31.

Berglund, Jeff. "'Planting the Seeds of Revolution': An Interview with Poet Esther Belin (Diné)." *Studies in American Indian Literatures* Ser. 2, 17 (2005): 62–72.

Berry, Wendell. *The Unsettling of America: Culture and Agriculture.* San Francisco: Sierra Club, 1977.

"Between Four Sacred Mountains: The Diné and the Land in Contemporary America." http://xroads.virginia.edu/~MA97/dinetah/front.html.

De Ramirez, Susan Berry Brill. "Introduction: 'A Spring Wind Rising ... Listen. You Can Hear It.'" *Studies in American Indian Literatures* Ser. 2, 16 (2004): 3–8.

Funsten, Kenneth. "100 Books for the Modern Person." *Los Angeles Times*, Sep. 20 1981: Book Section 3. "100 Books for the Modern Person by Kenneth Funsten (*Los Angeles Times*)." http://www.interleaves.org/~rteeter/grtlat.html.

Glancy, Diane. "He Has More Than One Ear." *Studies in American Indian Literatures* Ser. 2, 7 (1995): 1–2.

Jaskoski, Helen. "Thinking Woman's Children and the Bomb." *Explorations in Ethnic Studies* 13 (July, 1990): 1–24.

Jones, Mike. "This Is What It Means . . . A Conversation with *Smoke Signals* Writer Sherman Alexie." http://indiewire.com/people/int_Alexie_ Sherman_980116. html.

Kaufman, Francine Ratner. *Diabestiy: The Obesity-Diabetes Epidemic That Threatens America—And What We Must Do to Stop It.* New York: Bantam, 2005.

Kennedy, Virginia. "Unlearning the Legacy of Conquest: Possibilities for *Ceremony* in the Non-Native Classroom." *American Indian Culture and Research Journal* 28 (2004): 76.

Mahfouz, Naguib. "Zaabalawi." *The Norton Anthology of World Literature.* Ed. Sarah Lawall et al. 2nd ed. 6 vols. New York: Norton, 2002. 6: 2531–38.

Melville, Herman. "Bartleby the Scrivener." *The Piazza Tales and Other Prose Pieces* Chicago: Northwestern University Press, 1987. 13–45.

Mooney, James. *Myths of the Cherokee. 19th Annual Report of the Bureau of American Ethnology, 1897–98.* Washington: Bureau of American Ethnology, 1900. Part 1: 327–29.

Nelson, Robert M. "Settling for Vision in Silko's *Ceremony*: Sun Man, Arrowboy, and Tayo." *American Indian Culture and Research Journal* 28 (2004): 67–73.

———. "Rewriting Ethnography: The Embedded Texts in Leslie Silko's *Ceremony.*" *Telling the Stories: Essays on American Indian Literatures and Cultures.* Ed. Elizabeth Hoffman Nelson and Malcolm A. Nelson. New York: Peter Lang, 2001. 47–58.

Orr, David W. *The Nature of Design: Ecology, Culture, and Human Intention.* New York: Oxford University Press, 2002.

Ortiz, Simon J. *Men on the Moon..* Tucson: University of Arizona Press, 1999.

———, ed. *Speaking for the Generations: Native Writers on Writing.* Tucson: University of Arizona Press, 1998.

———. *Woven Stone.* Tucson: University of Arizona Press, 1992.

Owens, Louis. *Other Destinies: Understanding the American Indian Novel.* Norman: University of Oklahoma Press, 1992.

Palmer, Parker J. "The Grace of Great Things: Reclaiming the Sacred in Knowing, Teaching, and Learning,.." *The Heart of Learning: Spirituality in Education.* Ed. Steven Glazer. New York: Tarcher/Penguin, 1999. 15–32.

Penner, Andrea M. "The Moon Is So Far Away: An Interview with Luci Tapahonso," *Studies in American Indian Literatures* Ser. 2, 8 (1996): 1–12.

Premchand (Dhanpat Rai Shrivastava), "Zaabalawi," *The Norton Anthology of World Literature*. Ed. Sarah Lawall, et al. 2nd edition. 6 vols. New York: Norton, 2002. 6: 2531–38.

Rios, Alberto. "Some Extensions on the Sovereignty of Science," *The Smallest Muscle in the Human Body*. Port Townsend, WA: Copper Canyon, 2002.

Shaw, Anna Moore. *A Pima Past*. Tucson: University of Arizona Press, 1974.

Silko, Leslie Marmon. *Ceremony*. New York: Penguin, 1977.

———. "Yellow Woman," *The Norton Anthology of World Literature,* Ed. Sarah Lawall, et al. 2nd edition. 6 vols. New York: Norton, 2002. 6: 3143–50.

———. *Yellow Woman and a Beauty of the Spirit: Essays on American Life Today*. New York: Simon and Schuster, 1996.

Smith, Patricia Clark, with Paula Gunn Allen. "Earthly Relations, Carnal Knowledge: Southwestern American Indian Writers and Landscape," *"Yellow Woman,"* ed. Melody Graulich (New Brunswick, NJ: Rutgers University Press, 1993. 174–196.

Tapahonso, Luci. *Blue Horses Rush In*. Tucson: University of Arizona Press, 1997.

———. *Sáanii Dahataał: The Women Are Singing*. Tucson: University of Arizona Press, 1993.

Tompkins, Jane. *A Life in School: What the Teacher Learned*. Reading, MA: Perseus, 1996.

Webb, George. *A Pima Remembers*. Tucson: University of Arizona Press, 1959.

West, Dennis, and Joan West. "Sending Cinematic Smoke Signals: An Interview with Sherman Alexie," *Cineaste* 23 (1998): 28-33. http://www.lib.berkeley.edu/MRC/alexie.html. March 8, 2006.

Further Readings

Brown, Dee Alexander. *Bury My Heart at Wounded Knee: An Indian History of the American West.* New York: Holt, Rinehart & Winston, 1971. Though Brown's work was never given its due in academic circles, this book has changed the way many readers, both European Americans and American Indians, viewed the history of the United States. In particular, it has been given credit for contributing to the "Pan-Indian" movement by helping American Indian peoples see the widespread nature of abuses and mistreatment.

Black Elk, and John G. Neihardt. *Black Elk Speaks.* Lincoln: University of Nebraska Press, 1988. This book might be described as required reading for anyone who wants to teach American Indian literature. Though there are complex questions about its origins (Black Elk's words were translated by his son, written down in English by Neihardt's daughter, and then revised by Neihardt), Vine Deloria, Jr., points out in his introduction to the 1979 edition that to young American Indians, "the book has become a North American bible of all tribes" (xii).

Chavkin, Allan, ed. *Leslie Marmon Silko's* Ceremony: *A Casebook.* New York: Oxford University Press, 2002. This is a very useful survey of recent criticism on a text that is central to American Indian (and American) literature. Though some of the essays are more directly useful to the scholar than to the teacher, the collection offers a good overview of approaches to a very complex novel.

Goebel, Bruce A. *Reading Native American Literature: A Teacher's Guide.* Urbana, IL: National Council of Teachers of English, 2004. Goebel does a good job in his first chapter of reviewing the cultural and ethical issues involved in the teaching of American Indian literature by and for non-Indians. His approach is based on educating the reader about the two cultures (Blackfeet and Pueblo) that form the context for James Welch's *Fools Crow* and Leslie Marmon Silko's *Ceremony.* He includes definitions of terms and useful dsecriptions of customs and ceremonies. The book could serve as a very helpful background to anyone teaching these novels or other works.

Kabotie, Michael (Lomawywesa). *Migration Tears.* Los Angeles: American Indian Studies Center, 1987. Though Kabotie is better known as an artist and silversmith, this little book of poems captures his trickster's sense of humor and his considerable ability to craft images. It also helps to fill a gap, as there is not very much poetry by traditional Hopis available.

Lame Deer, John (Fire), and Richard Erdoes. *Lame Deer, Seeker of Visions*. New York: Touchstone, 1973. Lame Deer and Erdoes have created a vivid, informative, bawdy, and utterly captivating book. It will demolish student stereotypes of the "solemn Indian" and show them that our culture's view of the "medicine man" is completely inadequate. In addition, it introduces an American Indian way of seeing in straightforward and entertaining prose. I often use chapter 5, "The Circle and the Square," to introduce students to differences between American India cultures and our own.

Loftin, John. "A Religious Practicality." *Religion and Hopi Life in the Twentieth Century*. Bloomington: Indiana University Press, 1994. 3–13. This is an excellent background source. Loftin's work is careful and sensitive, and he gives a clear sense of the importance of spirituality in the everyday life of Hopis. The first chapter, "A Religious Practicality," is especially helpful.

Morrison, Dane, ed. *American Indian Studies: An Interdisciplinary Approach to Contemporary Issues*. New York: Peter Lang, 1997. This book is impressive in its scope and inclusiveness. There are essays here from many perspectives—literary, historical, sociological, archaeological, and so on. It can give students a sense of the variety of approaches that can be brought to bear on the study of literature and culture.

Viehmann, Martha L. "Settings, Place, Time, and Navajo Culture in Selections from Luci Tapahonso's *Sáanii Dahataał: The Women Are Singing*." *Kentucky Philological Review* 18 (2004): 48–54. There are not many essays that focus solely on Tapahonso, and this is a good one. As the title suggests, Viehmann focuses on the poetry in its cultural context and does an excellent job of relating the literature to the place and the traditions.

Zepeda, Ofelia. *Ocean Power: Poems from the Desert*. Tucson: University of Arizona Press, 1995. Zepeda is a linguist as well as a poet, and the book includes poems in English, in Tohono O'Odham, and in a mixture of both languages. There is not much poetry available from the O'Odham peoples, so this is a valuable resource that can supplement George Webb's *A Pima Remembers*.

www.ingramcontent.com/pod-product-compliance
Ingram Content Group UK Ltd.
Pitfield, Milton Keynes, MK11 3LW, UK
UKHW021834140426
5217IPUK00021B/1439